EZRA
and
NEHEMIAH

A COMMENTARY

by

G. COLEMAN LUCK

MOODY PRESS

CHICAGO

CONTENTS

:

EZRA

OUTLINE

1. ZERUBBABEL LEADS THE FIRST RETURN FROM EXILE AND
   REBUILDS THE TEMPLE (1:1—6:22)

   Cyrus Issues His Decree (1:1-4)

   A Group of Israelites Prepares To Return (1:5-11)

   The Exiles Return to the Land (2:1-70)

   The Altar Is Built and the Temple Foundation
   Laid (3:1-13)

   Samaritan Opposition Causes Suspension of the Work
   (4:1-24)

   The Work Is Begun Again Because of the Encouragement
   of Haggai and Zechariah (5:1-17)

   King Darius Confirms the Decree of Cyrus and the
   Temple Is Completed (6:1-22)

2. EZRA LEADS THE SECOND EXPEDITION FROM EXILE AND
   RECALLS THE PEOPLE TO THEIR SEPARATED POSITION
   (7:1—10:44)

   A Second Remnant Prepares To Return Under Ezra's
   Leadership (7:1-28)

   Ezra and His Company Journey to and Arrive in Jerusalem (8:1-36)

   Ezra Finds the People Have Lost Their Separated Position (9:1-4)

   Ezra Carries the Matter to God in a Great Prayer of
   Confession (9:5-15)

   Revival Begins (10:1-8)

   The People Return to Their Separated Position (10:9-44)

BACKGROUND

The human writer of the Old Testament book of Ezra is not specifically stated but traditionally has been thought to have been Ezra himself. No valid reason has yet been offered for doubting his authorship. The fact that he sometimes speaks of himself in the first person and sometimes in the third (7:1, 11, 25, 28; 8:15-17, 21, etc.) should not be thought of as militating against this long-held view. Daniel does the same thing, as do certain Gentile writers of that period.

As in the case of other Bible personalities, Ezra's name—"the helper"—well fits his character. He was indeed a true helper of God and also of his own people. Ezra was a priest, his father being named Seraiah (7:1). In addition he calls himself a scribe (7:6, 21), which he evidently considered his chief occupation. In that day the scribes were, as the name indicates, the copyists of the sacred Scriptures. But they were much more, they were also the recognized teachers and authorities on the law. Their time was principally spent in the study and interpretation of the Old Testament. Because in Israel religious and civil law were one and the same, the scribes are sometimes called lawyers in the New Testament.[1] The Lord Jesus generally condemned them as hypocrites (see Matt. 23; Mark 12:38-40; Luke 20:45-47;

---

[1] "*Lawyer* (Gr. *nomikos*, according to *law*), a term used to signify one who is *conversant with the law*, 'jurist' (Matt. 22:35; Luke 7:30; 10:25; 11:45; 14:3; Tit. 3:13), and probably applied to a scribe (*q.v.*) in his practical administration of the law in the pronunciation of legal decisions. It is not accidental that the expression is so frequently used by St. Luke. He purposes by the repetition to make clear to his Roman readers the character of the Jewish scribes" (Merrill F. Unger, *Unger's Bible Dictionary*, p. 651).

11:45-54). Not all of them, however, were such (Mark 12:28-34). Ezra himself was most assuredly a godly man (7:10).

Hebrew tradition says Ezra was high priest of his people before he left Babylon. He is said to have started the "Great Synagogue" and to have been the first president of that assembly which preceded the Sanhedrin as the supreme tribunal of the Jews. Tradition further attributes to him the collecting of the Old Testament books and the setting of the canon of that portion of Scripture, in addition to the institution of the synagogue worship system. He is supposed to have lived to a ripe old age and to have died while on a trip to the court of Artaxerxes in Persia. It is said that he was then buried at Samarah on the lower Tigris River.[2] There is no way of knowing for certain whether these extra-biblical pieces of information are completely accurate.

DATE

Ezra's book, in the events which it describes, covers more time than is apparent at first reading. The story begins with the decree of Cyrus permitting the Jews to return to their land (1:1-3), and ends shortly after Ezra's arrival in Jerusalem (7:7-9; 10:17). Therefore the book covers a period of about eighty years (538-457 B.C.). Between the close of chapter 6 and the opening of chapter 7 evidently about fifty-seven years elapsed. The book itself no doubt was written shortly after the time of the scene with which it closes.

[2] *Pulpit Commentary,* VII, iv.

Languages

Ezra's book, like that of Daniel, was originally written in two languages. There are certain sections in Aramaic (4:7— 6:18; 7:12-26). The balance is in Hebrew. The Aramaic language is directly alluded to in Ezra 4:7; Daniel 2:4; II Kings 18:26 and Isaiah 36:11. In these texts the Authorized Version uses the translation "Syriack" or "Syrian." The American Standard Version does the same, but adds in the margin either "Aramaic" or "Aramean." The Hebrew word used is *Aramith*. *Aram* ("the high land") is the Hebrew name for Syria. The various Semitic languages of the ancient Near East were closely related. Scholars divide them into two main groups: the East Semitic and the West Semitic. *"East Semitic* includes but one main language, Akkadian, divided into the slightly differing dialects of Babylonian and Assyrian. . . . *West Semitic* . . . comprises Ugaritic, Phoenician and Canaanite (of which Hebrew and Moabite are dialects)."[3] East Semitic is said to be the basis of the Syriac language of the Christian era, and West Semitic the basis of biblical Aramaic as found in Daniel and Ezra. "Recent discoveries of fifth century Aramaic documents, however, have shown quite conclusively that Daniel was, like Ezra, written in a form of Imperial Aramaic, an official or literary dialect which had currency in all parts of the Near East."[4] This Aramaic is said to have been "the predominant language spoken by the heterogeneous population of this metropolis [Babylon]."[5]

While various theories have been suggested, the precise

[3] Gleason L. Archer, Jr., *A Survey of Old Testament Introduction*, p. 12.
[4] *Ibid.*, p. 376.
[5] *Ibid.*, p. 378.

reason as to why Daniel and Ezra wrote their books partly in each language is not known.[6]

PURPOSE

> The Book of Ezra is a work of so simple a character as scarcely to require an "Introduction." It is a plain and straightforward account of one of the most important events in Jewish history—the return of the people of God from the Babylonian captivity. This return had two stages. . . . Very little that is directly didactic occurs in it: the writer tells his story as plainly as he can, and leaves his story to teach its own lessons.[7]

Observe that in presenting its picture of the reestablishment of the Jews in their land following the Babylonian captivity, the book records two distinct returns. The first was under the leadership of Zerubbabel (chaps. 1-6). Then seventy-eight years later the second took place under Ezra himself (chaps. 7-10). In these two sections, 2:1 and 6:21-22 make suitable key verses. The key word (or key expression) of the book is the frequently used "go up" or "went up." Another key word is Jerusalem. The name of the city is used forty-seven times in the book of Ezra. This then is the account of the "going up" of the exiled Jews to Jerusalem to rebuild their temple and city, as well as to reestablish their land after the long seventy-year captivity in Babylon.

---

[6] Charles F. Pfeiffer, in a personal letter, makes the following statement: "That Aramaic became the common language of postexilic Judaism is clear enough (although the scrolls indicate that Hebrew was not dead by any means). At Qumran we have *both* Hebrew and Aramaic (as the Aramaic Midrash on Genesis). Justification for the use of both languages is easy to find—but just why one book should have parts of each is not easy to understand —at least I have no ideas. Perhaps some records were preserved in each language and the the, Biblical writers saw no reason to translate."

[7] *Pulpit Commentary,* VII, i, iii.

1

ZERUBBABEL LEADS THE FIRST RETURN FROM EXILE AND REBUILDS THE TEMPLE (1:1–6:22)

The first personage presented to us in the book is Cyrus, king of Persia. Cyrus the Great came to the throne of Anshan, a region of Elam (just west of Persia proper), about 559 B.C. He commenced a long series of military conquests by taking Media. Eventually he controlled an empire from the Aegean Sea to India. The empire he founded lasted about two centuries, being finally conquered by Alexander the Great. "The first year" mentioned in the opening verse does not refer to the very beginning of his reign but to the first year of his control of Babylon, which he conquered approximately 539 B.C. Soon after this he granted permission to the Jews to return to their homeland.

A famous cylinder by Cyrus, found in the nineteenth century, indicates that he also allowed other captive peoples to go back to their native lands, thus totally reversing the policy of the preceding empires of Assyria and Babylon.

> Archaeological evidence that Cyrus pursued a liberal and tolerant policy toward deported peoples, such as the Jews whom he found in Babylonia, was discovered during the nineteenth century by Rassam, who found the Cyrus Cylinder. This cylinder states concerning such groups, "All of

13

their peoples I assembled and restored to their own dwelling-places." A picture of one of Cyrus' cylinders appears in several handbooks on archaeology. It tells of his taking the city of Babylon without violence, and later, of returning people to their former dwellings.[1]

Scores of years before Cyrus captured Babylon — at the very time of Nebuchadnezzar's conquest of Judah — the Prophet Jeremiah had foretold that the captivity of the Jews would last for seventy years (Jer. 25:12; 29:10). Various features however would have prevented the Bible student of that day from perfect certainty as to the conclusion of this period. The exact point of beginning of the seventy years was a matter of question. Did the period date from the time Nebuchadnezzar first gained control of Jerusalem, or from the time of its destruction twenty years later? At least a small difference could also have been made by the type of year used. Was it a "prophetic year" of 360 days (see Rev. 11:2-3; 12:6, 14), or a solar year of 365 days? Daniel, in the closing year of Belshazzar's reign, realized that the time must be nearly concluded (Dan. 8:1). Before that year had come to an end, Babylon had been captured by Cyrus as described in Daniel 5. It seems clear now that God's dating began with the first capture of Jerusalem in 606 B.C. This was the occasion when Daniel himself, with others, was carried to Babylon.

Read again these opening verses of Ezra to see the manner in which the Lord fulfilled His prophecy. He "stirred up the spirit of Cyrus." Almost two centuries earlier, Isaiah had marvelously predicted this, even calling Cyrus by name long before his birth (Isa. 44:28—45:6). The Jewish histor-

[1] Joseph P. Free, *Archaeology and Bible History*, p. 237.

ian Josephus wrote that Cyrus was actually shown these words from Isaiah, hinting that the great king had an interview with Daniel after the conquest of Babylon.[2] This may well be true, but the basic reason, after all, that King Cyrus issued his beneficent decree was because God stirred up his spirit. This surely demonstrates the fact that God, in His majestic sovereignty, can work even in the hearts of the unsaved to cause them to accomplish His will, thereby working out the good of His people (Rom. 8:28).

It would be interesting to know the exact religious experience of Cyrus, but there are no details. In this decree he undoubtedly showed that he knew there was one supreme God, whom he plainly identified with Jehovah, the God of Israel. He also clearly understood that his own authority had come to him from Jehovah, and knew that he had been appointed to accomplish a special task for the Lord.

Therefore this proclamation was sent throughout his empire, being announced vocally by heralds at various places and also posted in written form throughout the land. In it an important question was asked by the king: "Who is there among you of all his people?" This would include not only the tribe of Judah but all the ten tribes, for all were "Jehovah's people." The area to which the Assyrians had transported the ten tribes was a part of Cyrus' realm. Though the majority of those who accepted the invitation and returned were from Judah, it seems clear that some from the other tribes accompanied them.

Not only were the Israelites given permission to return to Jerusalem but they were *commanded* to rebuild the temple there. The reference in the first part of verse 4 is to the

[2] Josephus, *Antiquities of the Jews*, XI. 1. 2.

Israelites who yet sojourned in any part of the empire. Their Gentile neighbors were asked to help any who were poor in their arrangements for this return trip by providing them with money, goods and beasts. They were also permitted to send with the Jews freewill offerings for the house of God. The whole decree verifies that which secular historians have said regarding Cyrus — that he was a man of a noble and kindly character who sought to act the part of a father to his subjects.

A GROUP OF ISRAELITES PREPARES TO RETURN (1:5-11)

Following the publication of the king's edict, by no means all of the Israelites decided to return to their native land. Their exile had not been anything like the length of that of the modern Jews, nevertheless it had been many years since they had been forced to leave their homeland. Most of the Jews returning to Israel in the twentieth century have come from nations in which they suffered persecution at least in some degree. But from countries like the United States, where they have enjoyed relative prosperity, very few have turned to the new nation of Israel, founded in 1948. All the people were willing to leave Egypt in Moses' day for they had been bitterly used as slaves. Under Babylonian and Persian rule, however, not all had been enslaved. Many had prospered materially and had gained possessions they were not eager to leave. Others probably feared the risks involved in traveling to a land they had not personally seen, where they would have to start a pioneer work of rebuilding a desolate country.

Some, however, "rose up" immediately and made preparations to return. Among the first of these were to be found certain outstanding leaders of the tribes of Judah and Benjamin, in whose territory the capital city Jerusalem had stood. A group of priests and Levites joined them. Their particular interest was naturally in Jerusalem as the religious center of the land, since they would officiate in the restored house of God that Cyrus had commanded to be built. Other lesser people from the various tribes volunteered to go along and take part in the work of reconstruction.

The Scripture makes it clear that it was not a merely natural movement due simply to the fact that some were content to stay, while others being dissatisfied with their condition were willing to try anything new. God touched the spirits of certain ones, putting it into their hearts to want to go. How good it is to learn that those whom He touched responded!

The neighbors of those who decided to leave assisted them with money, beasts, equipment and "precious things" (v. 6). These helpers apparently included both the Israelites who remained behind and also their Gentile acquaintances, even as the Egyptians long before had contributed to the departing Israelites (Exodus 12:35-36).

Cyrus himself produced the original temple vessels and bestowed them upon the returning exiles. These had been carried away by Nebuchadnezzar, some at the time of his first capture of Jerusalem, the balance on the occasion of his destruction of the temple (cf. II Chron. 36:7, 10; Dan. 1:2). They had been desecrated by the impious Belshazzar who had been judged for his sin by the handwriting on the wall (Dan. 5:2-3). While this gift of temple vessels was comparatively a small thing, it probably tremendously encouraged the company of pioneers. Remember that their worship was much more formal than our own. To have these sacred vessels restored for the first time in many years to their proper owners was a real token of the blessing of God on their enterprise.

These valued utensils were committed to Sheshbazzar, prince of Judah (v. 8), who evidently was the expedition's recognized leader. His Babylonian name is thought to mean "sungod, guard the Lord." [3] It seems to be beyond question another name for Zerubbabel ("seed of Babylon").[4] Shesh-bazzar is called "prince of Judah" (1:8). He is also called the "governor" (5:14). Zerubbabel is likewise called by both of these titles (Hag. 1:1; I Chron. 3:19; Matt. 1:11-12). Ezra 5:16 states that Sheshbazzar laid the foundation of the temple. Zechariah 4:9 says that Zerubbabel did this. Very clearly then both names—one Babylonian, the other Hebrew—refer to the same man.

In the closing verses of Ezra 1, the temple vessels are itemized. The various items mentioned in verses 9-10 add up to 2,499. The total, however, is said in verse 11 to be 5,400. Some commentators consider this to be the reflection of a copyist's error. Ancient interpreters explained the difference by stating that the 5,400 included many small pieces which were not itemized individually and were not included in the list previously given, which seems the more satisfactory solution of the problem.

The Exiles Return to the Land (2:1-70)

The Leaders of the Expedition (vv. 1-2a)

The opening verse sadly recalls that Judah was no longer

---

[3] Merrill F. Unger, *Unger's Bible Dictionary*, p. 1014.
[4] *Ibid.*, p. 1187.

a separate independent kingdom as in the happier days before the captivity. Now it had become "the province"—a province of Persia. It was simply a dependency, a tributary state under the supreme control of an outside ruler.

From the standpoint of age, the returnees were a thoroughly mixed group. There were in their number old men who had seen the first temple previous to its destruction some fifty years before (3:12). The company also included children, grandchildren, and doubtless even great-grandchildren of the Jews who had earlier gone into captivity. Though the group is spoken of as having "come again unto Jerusalem," not all of their number settled there. It is explicitly stated that they went "everyone unto his city." This means that the people settled in the various towns and villages where their families had originally lived.

The appointed leader of the entire company was Zerubbabel, the prince of Judah. The high priest was Jeshua, called elsewhere Joshua. Since the high priest was always a descendant of Aaron, Joshua was of course from the tribe of Levi. Verse 2, after recording the names of these two men, lists nine others, making a total of eleven. This group quite plainly comprised the chief leaders of the movement, as it is said the rest of the people came with them. Nehemiah, incorporating this same information in his own book, gives this identical list of chief men (Neh. 7:7), adding a twelfth name—Nahamani. It seems not only reasonable but inevitable that each of these men was a prince of one of the twelve tribes of Israel. The people later seemed to consider themselves as representing not just one or two tribes, but the entire twelve (see 2:70; 6:17; 8:35).

Besides Zerubbabel and Joshua, only two other names

in this list are familiar to Bible students—Nehemiah and Mordecai. However, it is evident that neither of these was the familiar personage bearing that name. The Nehemiah who is the leading character in the next book of the Bible was originally cupbearer to the king of Persia and first came to Judah as governor about eighty years after this original expedition. Mordecai, the relative of Esther, was an elderly man who remained in Persia and subsequently became prime minister there.

The Returnees According to Families (vv. 2b-16)

This chapter does not of course name every individual in this returning company. However, the total is divided in several ways. First, certain of the people are listed according to families. Remember that ever since Israel became a nation there had been large and distinct family groups within the various tribes (see Num. 3:17-20).

The Returnees According to Cities (vv. 17-35)

In this section cities rather than families are named. Apparently the division begins with verse 17. Certainly a number of names that follow are cities, such as Bethlehem, Anathoth, Ramah, Bethel, Ai. It is not known why some of the people were listed by families and others by cities.

The Priests (vv. 36-39)

The total number of priests who returned was 4,289, divided according to four families. The high priest Joshua appears to have come from the first of these. All the family names mentioned in these verses are in previous Old Testament accounts of the priests of Israel.

The Levites (vv. 40-42)

The division here is threefold: the Levites proper who directly assisted the priests, the temple singers and the porters. The total number comprised only 341. Especially small was the group of just 74 Levites to assist the more than 4,000 priests.

The Nethinim and the Descendants of Solomon's Servants (vv. 43-58)

The word Nethinim is said to mean "those given." [5] These people are thought to have been the descendants of the Gibeonites who made a treaty with the Israelites (Joshua 9) and became "hewers of wood and drawers of water." It is quite possible that later other prisoners of war were added to this group.

C. F. Keil states that Solomon's servants were wartime captives from other nations, besides the Canaanites, who were assigned to assist with the upkeep of the temple.[6] It is striking to observe that a considerable number of these people, after all the years of the captivity, still remained attached to the Israelites and returned to the land with them.

People Who Could Not Establish Their Genealogy (vv. 59-63)

It is not surprising that a number of Hebrews from several different sections of Babylon were unable to verify their descent. It is indeed far more astonishing that the genealogical records of so many Israelites had been preserved during the trying period of the exile than that in a few cases

---

[5] *Ibid.*, p. 790.

[6] C. F. Keil and Franz Delitzsch, *Biblical Commentary on the Old Testament*, VIII, 40.

this information had been lost. Among this group of those who could not authenticate their ancestry the ones most grievously affected were certain of the priests. Their case was brought to the governor himself.[7] His final ruling on the matter was that such should not be allowed to have any part in the priestly ministry or support until an authoritative high priest could receive divine revelation regarding the problem. The Urim and Thummim (literally, "lights and perfections") were stones in the breastplate of the high priest, which at least in ancient times gave a communication of the divine will (see Exodus 28:30; Lev. 8:8; Num. 27:21; Deut. 33:8; I Sam. 28:6; Neh. 7:65). The exact way in which this was accomplished is a matter of conjecture now.

Just what happened later to these questionable priests is never stated in the Scriptures. Some Bible students think that when the full priestly ritual was set up, Joshua the high priest consulted the Urim and Thummim and decided the question. Others feel that when Zerubbabel made his statement he was not referring at all to the then high priest, but rather to the promised Messiah who would some day appear.

H. A. Ironside compares these hapless priests with some church members of our own day who are not sure about their "genealogy."[8] Many professing Christians lack assurance because they are not certain concerning their standing with God and are not sure that they have really been "born again" into the divine family.

Sum Total of the Returnees (vv. 64-65)

The entire company is said to have totaled 42,360 (v.

---

[7] He is called Tirshatha (v. 63), the root meaning of which is "His seventy."
[8] H. A. Ironside, *Notes on Ezra, Nehemiah and Esther*, p. 22.

64). The parallel listing in Nehemiah 7 gives exactly the same figure (Neh. 7:66). However, the actual total of all the separate numbers given in Ezra 2 is but 29,818. If the parallel lists in Ezra 2 and Nehemiah 7 are compared, it will be found that Ezra includes several family groups not mentioned in Nehemiah, while Nehemiah includes several not found in Ezra. It is surprising to note that if those groups mentioned in Nehemiah but not in Ezra are added to the latter's actual total the figure comes to 31,583. If in a similar manner Ezra's surplus is added to Nehemiah's numbers the total again comes to 31,583. This would still leave the total of the individual groups 10,777 less than the grand total stated in both books. Perhaps the best solution to this difference is that of one commentator who says these were "omitted because they did not belong to Judah and Benjamin, or to the priests, but to the other tribes."[9]

Servants totaling 7,337 are also listed, as well as 200 "singing men and women." Possibly these were singers from other tribes who were added to the temple choir, the Levitical singers not being sufficient to adequately care for the music.

The List of Beasts, and the Offerings of the Leaders for the Temple Work (vv. 66-70)

It is surprising that even the animals were numbered! Lists of names and numbers such as this chapter contains seem unutterably dull to many modern readers. But remember,

There is something peculiarly solemn about records such

[9] Samuel Davidson as cited by John W. Haley, *An Examination of the Alleged Discrepancies of the Bible,* p. 381.

as these. Many, yea, most of the names in them are for us only names, but God has not forgotten one of the persons once called by these names on earth, and "in that day" He will reward according to the work of each. Some too must "suffer loss" for opportunities neglected or half-hearted service. Nothing of good or ill shall be overlooked by Him who seeth not as man seeth, who looks not on the outward appearance but on the heart. How little did any of these devoted Jews of Ezra's day think that God would preserve a registry of their names and families for future generations to read, and thus to learn how highly He values all that is done from devotion of heart to Himself and for the glory of His name! [10]

The Altar Is Built and the Temple Foundation Laid (3:1-13)

It was stated in chapter 2 that the exiles returned "everyone unto his city." Doubtless the first thing these people did was to build shelters for their families and make other arrangements for their living in the new land. By the time the events of chapter 3 took place obviously some time had elapsed, though it is not known exactly how long. But here it is told how the altar was set up and put in use (vv. 1-3).

In the seventh month, the people "as one man" (v. 1) gathered in Jerusalem. This was a great religious month for Israel, for in it the last three of their annual religious festivals were scheduled—the Feast of Trumpets on the first day of the month, the Day of Atonement on the tenth day, and the Feast of Tabernacles from the fifteenth to the twenty-first day. Perhaps the arrival of this month with its three notable celebrations turned the minds of the people

[10] Ironside, pp. 18-19.

to spiritual matters. But it is evident that underneath it all there was an unseen working of God causing all of them suddenly to decide to gather in Jerusalem.

When this divine movement was upon the people as a whole, the hearts of the leaders were also responsive to the Spirit of God. The high priest, with the lesser priests, and the governor, with "his brethren," stood up and built the altar of burnt offerings. They determined not to wait until the entire temple had been rebuilt (which proved to be even farther in the future than they then realized) but go ahead with the most essential feature of all their worship ritual— the sacrifices.

The high priest Jeshua is called Joshua in Haggai and Zechariah. Jesus is the corresponding Greek form of the name. Joshua's father was Jozadak (or Jehozadak) and his grandfather Seraiah (I Chron. 6:14-15). This Seraiah was high priest at the time Nebuchadnezzar destroyed Jerusalem. The downfall of the city had been the occasion for his own execution (II Kings 25:18-21). Zerubbabel the governor was of course a descendant of David. His "brethren" were no doubt other members of the Davidic family.

In building their altar, these men did not follow any recent altar styles they may have observed, but they went back to the specifications given in the Mosaic law (Exodus 27:1-8). In the present age, Jesus Christ is said to be our "altar" (Heb. 13:10). On the Old Testament altar, the sacrifices symbolized Him and His atoning work. "Whenever the Spirit of God sends a true recovery and revival He will make the Lord Jesus Christ and His blessed finished work the first thing." [11]

[11] A. C. Gaebelein, *The Annotated Bible*. Vol. III: *Ezra-Psalms*, p. 13.

No sooner was the altar completed than it was set up and sacrifices offered upon it. The oblations offered were the morning and evening sacrifices of the continual burnt offering (see Exodus 29:38-42). H. A. Ironside has entitled a little book of devotional thoughts for the beginning and close of the day, *The Continual Burnt Offering*. This suggests that though we today do not offer animal sacrifices we can meditate each morning and evening on the Lord Jesus and His work for us.

The principal reason for their hurry in getting the sacrificial ritual started is said to have been "fear . . . of the people of those countries" (v. 3). In the early days of their return, the Jews were having trouble with their Gentile neighbors who resented their coming, just as did the Arabs in the twentieth century. This made the Hebrews realize keenly their need of divine help and protection and of getting right with God. Human nature is still the same today, for it often takes trials and tribulations to make us realize our need of divine assistance.

Next is recorded the observance of the Feast of Tabernacles and the first preparations for the construction of the temple (vv. 4-7). After the good beginning had been made of rebuilding the altar, it was decided to keep the Feast of Tabernacles, then due, exactly as prescribed in the law (Num. 29:12-38). This feast spoke in a prophetic way of the millennial blessing which will yet be granted to Israel when God's ancient people finally turn to their Messiah and are restored to their separated position.[12] The return of this small group of exiles can be thought of as prefiguring that great future event. It was thus very fitting that they

[12] See G. Coleman Luck, *The Bible Book by Book*, p. 27.

should begin their religious life with the observance of this particular feast.

This accomplished, they reinstituted the daily sacrifices, the monthly offerings and all the seven set feasts of the Lord. All this activity demonstrates that they had a real desire to be obedient to the law of God, and to please Him. Also they commenced again to offer the freewill offerings— sacrifices not required but brought entirely out of thankfulness to God for His mercy and goodness (cf. Lev. 22:17-25, et. al.).

The above mentioned things were accomplished before even the foundation of the temple had been laid. However, definite preparations were soon underway for the rebuilding of the house of God. Among the people were some who had learned the trades of masonry and carpentry in Babylon. Certain of these were engaged to work on the temple, and a money advance was given to them. Many materials for the original Solomonic temple had been supplied by Hiram, the king of Tyre (II Chron. 2). Now arrangements were made with the inhabitants of that same region to provide some of their famous cedar trees for the new structure. Since Tyre and Sidon did not produce sufficient victuals for themselves, payment was made to them in food, drink and oil. Probably King Cyrus had made a monetary grant to take care of at least a part of these expenses.

At the time of the actual laying of the foundation for the new temple, a special celebration was held (vv. 8-13). But before the work on the new edifice began, seven more months elapsed and the second year and the second month had arrived (about our May). Perhaps the precise date was chosen because it was the same time Solomon had begun the first temple (I Kings 6:1).

The task of superintending and overseeing the work was assigned to the Levites who energetically prosecuted their commission. The whole number of Levites was divided into the three family groups named in verse 9. Jeshua was not the high priest, but rather the Levite mentioned in 2:40.

At the moment the work was ready to begin, a special religious service was held. Music was supplied by the sons of Asaph, who sang together "by course" (antiphonally). From the selection quoted it seems likely that they used Psalm 118. At the completion of this service all the people shouted out their praise of God "with a loud shout" (v. 13).

Many of the leaders present were "ancient men" (v. 12) and had vivid recollections of the original temple. Since that edifice had only been destroyed fifty or fifty-five years before this date, some present could easily have seen it. While the younger people shouted for joy over the commencement of the new temple, these older men wept. It is not directly stated as to why they wept but the reason was doubtless the same mentioned a bit later.[13] The new temple was not to be as large as had been Solomon's, nor was its foundation so costly. When King Solomon began his temple, the nation was at the peak of its glory and prosperity. This new temple was being built by a small minority of the nation—people who had just returned from captivity in a strange land. It is not hard to understand why the new temple was not as costly or as beautiful as its predecessor. So some wept while others joyfully shouted, and these two

---

[13] "Who is left among you that saw this house in her first glory? And how do ye see it now? Is it not in your eyes in comparison of it as nothing?" (Hag. 2:3).

diverse noises mingled together to make one great sound.

Old men are often inclined to be too pessimistic and to look too much to the past, sometimes unduly dampening the godly enthusiasm of the young by their attitude. But young people sometimes have a tendency to be overconfident and rush rashly ahead without proper preparation, thus making a miserable failure. In proper bounds both the wisdom and conservatism of age along with the vigor and enthusiasm of youth can be used in the Lord's work. "There is room both for the weeping and the shouting." [14]

SAMARITAN OPPOSITION CAUSES SUSPENSION OF THE WORK
(4:1-24)

Assistance was then offered to the Jews but rejected by them (vv. 1-3). When the northern ten tribes of Israel had been carried into captivity, the Assyrians later transported various other conquered peoples into their territory. These intermarried with the few Israelites left and thus formed a mixed race (see II Kings 17:24, ff.). These heathen people were idol worshipers, but they combined some sort of worship of Jehovah to their idolatry, producing an eclectic religion.

When these Samaritans heard that the Jews were making substantial progress, they came to them with an offer of assistance. While outwardly pretending to be friendly and cooperative, in reality they were adversaries for their actual intention was to corrupt and damage the work. Their proposal sounded fair enough: "Let us build with you: for we seek your God, as ye do." However, this was but a half

[41] Ironside, p. 36.

truth. They did indeed worship Jehovah, but not as the Israelites did.

Observe that Zerubbabel, Joshua and the other leaders immediately saw through this ruse, absolutely refusing to compromise with these people, and unequivocally rejecting their help. It was their intention to worship and serve Jehovah God only and their work was strictly in accordance with the command given them by King Cyrus. Superficially it may seem that these men of God dealt in a hard, cold way with people who had kindly proffered their friendship. But if they had agreed to the Samaritan proposal, their whole godly project would have been utterly ruined. These intruders did not really know the Lord at all and would have soon contaminated the work with their worldly outlook. In all too short a time they would have led the Israelites back into idolatry, the sin which had previously caused the downfall of their ancestors.

The action of Zerubbabel and Joshua is an apt illustration of the command in II Corinthians 6:14: "Be ye not unequally yoked together with unbelievers." They well knew that the temple of God could have no "agreement" with idols (cf. II Cor. 6:16). Today some of God's children have blighted their lives and weakened their Christian testimony by allowing themselves to be "yoked together with unbelievers" in such things as marriage, business partnership, lodge and secret societies. Saddest of all, unbelievers have often been allowed to come into the churches and corrupt the spiritual work. All too often in Christendom, men have been allowed to serve as ministers and even as officials superintending large segments of the work, when they openly denied basic doctrines of the Christian faith, and obviously knew nothing of what it meant to be "born again" through faith in Christ.

After this rebuff, the adversaries openly opposed the work in various ways (vv. 4-6). Surely Satan was behind all this because when God's work is prospering, the devil is usually aroused to greater activity in his opposition. Now, as then, he sometimes works by trying to corrupt from the inside, while on other occasions he turns to open opposition from the outside. Ezra 4 shows that when the first method failed, Satan's servants adopted the second. By this they clearly demonstrated that they never had any real interest in the service of the Lord.

So these "people of the land" now did their best to hinder the labor. "To strengthen the hands" is an expression meaning to help, so "to weaken the hands" means just the opposite—to hinder. The exact ways by which they tried to accomplish this are not specified. However, their methods probably were similar to those later used against Nehemiah, with various schemes concocted to retard the construction of the temple. One of their devices was to hire counselors against the Jews. Such counselors would roughly correspond to lobbyists employed by special interests in the States and sent to Washington for the purpose of influencing officials and legislators. Generally there are courtiers in kingly courts who for a price will use their influence (either real or pretended) with the king. Such men worked to "frustrate their purpose" (v. 5) during the balance of the reign of King Cyrus, and even beyond that through the administrations of the three kings who succeeded him.

The king who immediately followed Cyrus was called Ahasuerus (v. 6), which seems to be a title rather than a proper name. According to Gesenius, this means king, being from a Persian word signifying "lion-king." As recorded in secular history, the actual name of this monarch was Cambyses, the son of Cyrus. He "possessed his father's adventurous spirit without his commanding genius." [15] Having pestered Cyrus without effect during the closing years of his reign, these adversaries immediately approached Cambyses as soon as he had taken office. They sent him a letter accusing the Jews of various crimes. Like his father, he evidently paid no attention to the complaint, knowing that the permission to rebuild had been granted the Jews by King Cyrus.

Later the adversaries sent another complaint during the reign of Artaxerxes (vv. 7-10). The name Artaxerxes, like Ahasuerus, was a title rather than a proper name, said to mean "great king." [16] This Artaxerxes is evidently the man whom historians now call Pseudo-Smerdis.

> Cambyses, the son of Cyrus, had his younger brother Smerdis assassinated. While Cambyses was away on an expedition to Egypt, an impostor who bore a likeness to Smerdis, declared himself king. Cambyses started home to deal with this "Pseudo-Smerdis," but died on the way. The impostor reigned seven months before meeting his own death. Then the son-in-law of Cyrus, Darius Hystaspes, became monarch.[17]

This Darius Hystaspes is the ruler mentioned in Ezra 4:5, 24.

> Smerdis, son of Cyrus, was put to death by order of

[15] Unger, p. 239.
[16] Robert Young, *Analytical Concordance of the Bible*, p. 52.
[17] Luck, *Daniel*, pp. 113-14.

Cambyses, his brother. Patizithes, a Magian, had been left in charge of the palace of Cambyses and, taking advantage of the likeness of his own brother to Smerdis, proclaimed him king. Cambyses heard of this in Syria, but was killed by an accidental wound. The Persians acknowledged the false king and he reigned 7 months without opposition. Phaedima discovered the deception and told her father, Otanes, who with six noble Persians entered the palace and killed the bogus Smerdis and his brother in 521 B.C.[18]

Phaedima was first a wife of Cambyses, and later of the Pseudo-Smerdis.

During the time this Pseudo-Smerdis (Artaxerxes) was reigning, a special letter of accusation against the Jews was prepared. The writers of this communication were "Bishlam, Mithredath, Tabeel, and the rest of their companions" (v. 7). Just who these individuals were is not known, but obviously they were men of importance. It has been suggested that perhaps they were the deputy governors over all the provinces of the Medo-Persian Empire west of the Euphrates River.[19] Rehum the chancellor and Shimshai the scribe were also named as writers of this letter. Apparently Rehum was the governor of Samaria, and Shimshai was his executive secretary.

The expression "the rest of their companions" is explained in verse 9. Various nationalities are mentioned which had been brought to Samaria at the time of the deportation of the ten tribes. No doubt the purpose in citing all these names was to impress the new king. The various peoples mentioned are stated to have been settled there by "the

[18] P. G. Woodcock, *Concise Dictionary of Ancient History*, p. 380.
[19] Robert Jamieson, A. R. Fausset, and David Brown, *A Critical and Explanatory Commentary on the Old and New Testaments*, II, 590.

great and noble Asnapper" (v. 10). "In 1875 it was first suggested by Gelzur that Asnapper is simply an Aramaean form of the Assyrian name Ashurbanipal. This view, which seems so strange at first sight, is now almost universally accepted." [20] Ashurbanipal was the grandson of Sennacherib (see Isa. 36-37) and has been called "the last great Assyrian monarch."

The expression "and at such a time" (v. 10), with which the letter closes, could better be rendered "and so forth" (ASV). This signifies that Ezra in preparing the book did not include the entire superscription of the accusation, considering that what he had already given was sufficient.

The body of the communication which the adversaries sent to Artaxerxes is found in verses 11-16. They commenced by speaking of the Jews as having come up from the Persian king "to us" (v. 12), expressing that the Hebrews had previously migrated from the locality where the king of Persia lived to the section where the Samaritans resided. They then accused the Jews of rebuilding "the rebellious and the bad city." This description was probably based on the fact that Jerusalem had several times rebelled against Nebuchadnezzar, being at the end destroyed for this activity. The Samaritans would have been in a good position to be well acquainted with this history. They claimed that the Jews had again built up the walls of Jerusalem, thus fortifying the city, which was a complete falsehood. The actual rebuilding of these walls was not accomplished for many years as the book of Nehemiah makes clear. But considering the source, such exaggerated claims are not surprising.

[20] Unger, p. 99.

Then the Samaritans went on to accuse the Jews of fortifying their city with the direct purpose of rebelling against the Persian king and refusing to pay him the various kinds of taxes required of them. This was a clever stroke calculated to hit the king where he would be hurt the most—in the pocketbook!

If a city in the midst of a strong, well-run empire fortified itself, that would indeed have a striking appearance of rebellion. But in a loosely controlled domain like that of Persia, cities needed fortifications to protect themselves against adjacent provinces and lawless marauders.

The officials penning the letter did their best to make it appear that their only motive was loyalty to the king. They claimed that having received their maintenance from him, they could not bear to see him dishonored without taking immediate steps to remedy the condition.

The king was urged to search the records of the previous monarchs. It appears to have been the custom of Persian rulers to have recorded in a book the empire's important affairs. Such a record played a prominent part in the events of the book of Esther (6:1-4). The adversaries felt that if the records were searched, their own previous complaints would very likely be found and possibly also reference to Jerusalem's rebellion against Nebuchadnezzar.

The climax of the accusation was reached with the charge that if Jerusalem were actually rebuilt and its walls established again, the Jews themselves would not only rebel against the Persian crown, but would also snatch away from the king all his domain "on this side the river" (v. 16). Some think that this was a reference to the Jordan River.

However, in the Old Testament "the river" is many times used for the great Euphrates River.[21] If the Samaritans meant the Euphrates, then their charge was indeed audacious. Not since the day of Solomon had Israel controlled land all the way to the Euphrates (see I Kings 4:21). Later they once made an attack under King Menahem on this section (II Kings 15:16).[22]

The answer from Artaxerxes (vv. 17-22) was not long in coming. Though Cyrus and Ahasuerus (Cambyses) had apparently ignored the complaints addressed to them, Artaxerxes (Pseudo-Smerdis) quickly replied. Being an impostor and actually a heathen priest, he would be quite naturally inclined to oppose both what Cyrus had done and also the religious revival of Judaism. After indicating that the Samaritan letter had been read in his presence, he told how he then searched as they had suggested. The result was that he discovered from Persian records that Jerusalem had indeed rebelled against kings in former times. The facts behind this statement were undoubtedly their several rebellions against Nebuchadnezzar and possibly also their defiance of the Assyrians.

Quite clearly the Persians possessed historical records that were thorough and accurate, for Artaxerxes even found accounts of "mighty kings" who had in past time ruled from Jerusalem all the way to the Euphrates River. This description would fit David and Solomon who did control all this

---

[21] "The references to it [the Euphrates] in Scripture are greatly more numerous than might be supposed, if one were to judge by the simple occurrence of the name; for it is not unfrequently styled merely 'the river' by way of eminence, or 'the great river,' being so much the largest with which the Israelites were acquainted, that in certain connections it was indicated with sufficient definiteness by such a general designation, Ezr. 4:10, 16; Ps. 72:8; 80.11; Isa. 8:7; 11:15, etc." (Patrick Fairbairn, *Imperial Standard Bible Encyclopedia*, II, 254).

[22] Tiphsah mentioned in this verse is said elsewhere to be on the western bank of the Euphrates (see I Kings 4:24).

part of the world, exacting tribute from various petty chief-
tains and kings in the area.

That which the Samaritans desired was granted them—
authority to force the Jews to cease from rebuilding Jerusalem. Artaxerxes directed that this should be done "until
another commandment shall be given from me" (v. 21b).
This does not mean he had any intention of ever changing
the edict. It is stated in Daniel 6:8 that the laws of the
Medes and Persians, once signed by the king, could not
henceforth be altered. So probably the king usually added
that phrase in order to admit the possibility of a different
decree later, if the king so desired. Obviously the Samaritans hardly needed the urging with which the king's letter
closed (v. 22).

The chapter ends with a depressing view of the cessation
of the work (vv. 23-24). When the adversaries received this
missive from the king they hastened with all speed to Jerusalem. Upon arrival they forced the Jews to cease their
work of rebuilding temple and city. This put the Hebrews
in a difficult position because if they had resisted, they
would have been guilty of open rebellion against the king
himself.

But while not minimizing the peril of their situation, it is
evident from Haggai's prophecy that their own enthusiasm
for the work had also waned. There is no evidence that
they carried the matter any further, either by prayer to
God or by petition to the king. We are forced to conclude
that they capitulated too easily. All too often believers in
our own day do the same, giving up with hardly a struggle
when opposition arises against the Lord's work.

For some time the work had been progressing at a slow

pace due to opposition and to the workers' waning enthusiasm. Now it ceased entirely for approximately eighteen
months or two years (determined from the fact that Smerdis
reigned less than a year, and the building began again in
the second year of the new king, Darius).

The Darius who succeeded Artaxerxes was not the person called Darius the Median (see Dan. 5:31), who appears
to have been either an uncle of Cyrus[23] or one of his chief
generals.[24] The present Darius was called Darius Hystaspes
in secular history. A son-in-law of Cyrus the Great, he
reigned for about thirty-five years, beginning in 521 B.C.
A man of great energy and activity, he quelled revolts and
even enlarged the empire of Cyrus, extending it to India
and Egypt. His accomplishments included the reorganiza-
tion of the administration of the kingdom, the establishment
of a postal system and reformation in taxation. He finally
suffered a defeat at the hand of the Greeks in the great
Battle of Marathon (490 B.C.). At the time he died (485)
he was preparing another expedition against Greece. His
son and successor was Xerxes, the Ahasuerus of the book
of Esther.[25] Most noteworthy of all in connection with
Bible history, Darius Hystaspes was very kind and concilia-
tory to the Jews.

THE WORK IS BEGUN AGAIN BECAUSE OF THE ENCOURAGEMENT OF HAGGAI AND ZECHARIAH (5:1-17)

Although the king who had forbidden the Jews to work

---

[23] Known to secular history as Cyaxares II.

[24] John C. Whitcomb, *Darius the Mede*, ably argues that this personage is to be identified with Gubaru (Greek, Gobryus) whom both Greek historians and cuneiform inscriptions refer to as having a "key role n the capture of Babylon and its subsequent administration." For a good brief discussion see Gleason L. Archer, Jr., *A Survey of Old Testament Introduction*, pp. 371-74.

[25] "Xerxes, the son of Darius I the Great, is undoubtedly the Ahasuerus of the book of Esther" (Unger, p. 31).

had been slain, and a new monarch was on the throne for more than a year, the people still made no attempt to rebuild. Discouragement prevailed even with the leaders, Zerubbabel and Joshua. The people excused themselves by saying that it just was not the right time to rebuild the temple (Hag. 1:2). Then God began to move and the work soon commenced again (vv. 1-2).

In the sixth month of the second year of Darius' reign, the Lord raised up a prophet, Haggai; then two months later another—Zechariah (see Zech. 1:1). These men were the first prophets granted to Israel since Daniel, some sixteen years before, in the third year of King Cyrus had been shown his final vision (Dan. 10:1). Haggai and Zechariah exhorted the people to commence again their work of rebuilding (Hag. 1:8). Assurance was given the Jews that if they obeyed this command of God, He would enable them to complete the edifice (Zech. 4:7-9). Special encouragement was given to the leaders, Joshua and Zerubbabel (Hag. 2:4).

The ministry of these servants of the Lord produced the desired result. The leaders resumed their activity, the people went to work with "the prophets of God helping them" (v. 2b), doubtless by commanding, exhorting and encouraging.

The renewal of the construction brought to Jerusalem an even higher official than the governor of Samaria—Tatnai, the governor of all the provinces on the west of the Euphrates River (vv. 3-5). Zerubbabel, as governor of Judah, was under the supervision of this official. The Samaritans probably complained to Tatnai and he came to determine for himself just what was going on. Shethar-boznai, who was probably his secretary, accompanied him.

The officials asked the Jews the source of their authority for rebuilding temple and wall. From the letter written later (see v. 13), it is evident that Zerubbabel informed them of the decree of Cyrus. When they asked the names of the leaders in the project, Zerubbabel took sole responsibility, using his Babylonian name of Sheshbazzar (see vv. 14ff.).

It is not known for certain as to why "we" is used in verse 4, "Then said we unto them . . . What are the names. . . ." Some think this reflects a slight error on the part of a later copyist and should read "they." Possibly this is part of a contemporary document incorporated into the record at this point by Ezra. There is no doubt that the next verse (v. 5) is a comment of Ezra himself. He indicates that "the eye of their God" was upon these Jews, providing them with the needed blessing and care, so no one was able to halt the building until the favorable reply had finally been received from King Darius. While they dispatched a letter to the king, the officials permitted the Jews to continue their work.

Verses 7-17 contain the text of the letter from Tatnai to Darius. The Apharsachites (v. 6) may have been his bodyguard. It can easily be seen that this letter, written by a Persian official, is considerably fairer to the Jews than that of the Samaritans in the previous chapter. False accusations, such as the Samaritans made, are conspicuous by their absence. Tatnai simply describes in an objective way how he came to Judea, how he found the temple being rebuilt with great stones and timber, how he observed that the work was progressing rapidly and was prospering. Especially striking is the title this man used for the temple—"the house of the great God" (v.8). While he may have believed in many deities, at least he recognized Jehovah as the supreme God.

Tatnai related that in answer to his questions the Jews had stated that they were "the servants of the God of heaven and earth" (v. 11), who were rebuilding the house of God which a great king of Israel (Solomon) had erected many years before. If they were servants of Jehovah, and He was the great God, the question would naturally arise as to why He had permitted the temple to be destroyed in the first place. This, explained to Tatnai in verse 12, was because the ancestors of these Jews had sinned against their God and had provoked Him to wrath. For this reason He allowed Nebuchadnezzar to raze the temple and deport the Hebrews into Babylonian captivity.

Their explanation went on to tell of the decree of Cyrus, especially emphasizing the fact that he had restored to them the holy vessels of the house of God, taken previously by Nebuchadnezzar. King Cyrus had personally instructed Sheshbazzar (Zerubbabel) to "take these vessels" and rebuild the temple "in his place" (v. 15), the reference being to the site where it formerly stood.

When he stated that the temple had been in construction ever since Zerubbabel laid the foundation, either Tatnai did not know about the interruption of the work, or else he viewed it as not worthy of particular notice. He did comment on the fact that despite the years of labor the temple was still not completed (v. 16). The king was asked to search the records to ascertain whether the report of the Cyrus decree was true, then to send word as to his pleasure in the matter.

KING DARIUS CONFIRMS THE DECREE OF CYRUS
AND THE TEMPLE IS COMPLETED (6:1-22)

Upon receipt of the letter from Tatnai, Darius moved into immediate action (vv. 1-5). First he searched in the record house at Babylon, but apparently found nothing there. The investigation was continued elsewhere, and at the palace in Achmetha (or Ecbatana, ASV marg.) the original decree of Cyrus was found. Ecbatana was a city of Media in which the Persian kings maintained a palace where they resided during a portion of each year. This decree, although omitting certain items of the public proclamation given in chapter 1, adds interesting details not found in the proclamation itself.

Cyrus had specified originally that the foundations be "strongly laid" (v. 3). The height of the building was to be 60 cubits. In Solomon's temple the holy place was 30 cubits high (I Kings 6:2), and the porch was 120 cubits high (II Chron. 3:4). The breadth of 60 cubits was in fact greater than that of the original temple, which was 20 cubits. The building was to be built with layers of stones and timbers, with all the cost to be paid out of the king's treasury. Evidently Cyrus had envisioned a larger building than was actually constructed. It also seems clear that the funds he had planned to provide were never actually bestowed. King Cyrus had especially wanted the temple vessels restored, probably because he knew the story of Belshazzar and the judgment that came on him when he desecrated these sacred utensils (see Dan. 5).

Darius' decree is in verses 6-12. It seems that only a portion of the letter he sent to Tatnai is given, as the beginning is quite abrupt, with his opening word "be ye far from thence." Tatnai and his associates were to remain "far from" Jerusalem in respect to any stoppage or hindering of the work. They were instructed to permit the governor, Zerubbabel, and his people to continue their labor of rebuilding the temple, in accordance with Cyrus' original decree. In addition, Darius made a decree of his own to facilitate the project. Expenses were to be granted to the workmen "of the tribute beyond the river" (v. 8), which was a certain amount of tax money customarily raised and forwarded to the Persian king as a tribute. The expenses of the workmen were to come from this sum, with the balance being then sent to Darius. In this way the people themselves would have no additional taxes to pay—the king would simply get less.

The king ordered that bullocks, rams and lambs—the animals used by the Jews in their sacrifices—were to be daily supplied to the priests for the oblations regularly offered in the temple. Wheat, oil and salt were also to be provided for use in the meal offerings, and wine for the drink offerings which accompanied the sacrifices. The reason behind the king's command for doing all this was that he wanted the priests to "pray for the life of the king, and of his sons" (v. 10). Darius, like Cyrus, evidently recognized the fact that the God of the Jews—Jehovah—was far more than a mere tribal god. He was the supreme God, the "God of heaven." The exact religious experience of King Darius is unknown. Possibly he acknowledged Jehovah as the supreme God and yet worshiped other deities. However, perhaps he and Cyrus, Darius the Mede and Nebuchadnezzar all came to the place where they exerted real faith in the true God and were really saved men.

As to the request of Cyrus for prayer for himself and his sons, it is said that "the Jews have always maintained the practice of praying for the civil ruler of any country in which they have had their abode." [26] Christians are commanded to do the same thing during the present age:

> I exhort therefore, that, first of all, supplications, prayers, intercessions, and giving of thanks, be made for all men; for kings, and for all that are in authority; that we may lead a quiet and peaceable life in all godliness and honesty. For this is good and acceptable in the sight of God our Saviour; who will have all men to be saved, and to come unto the knowledge of the truth (I Tim. 2:1-4).

An additional decree was added by Darius in order to enforce obedience to the previous one. Any person who altered the word of his command was to have wood from his house torn down and used for the purpose of crucifying the offender. According to authorities, the Persians are known to have practiced two kinds of crucifixion, either of which may have been in the mind of the king. In certain cases, the body of the criminal was impaled on a large piece of wood. In others, the victim was beheaded and his body then fastened on a sort of cross.[27]

Not only was there provision for the execution of the person who disobeyed the edict, but in addition his house was to be made into a "dunghill" (i.e., a privy). Beyond these stipulations, Darius called on God Himself to destroy anyone—either ruler or private individual—who should in the future "put to their hand to alter and to destroy this house of God which is at Jerusalem" (v. 12). It has been

[26] *Pulpit Commentary*, VII, 81.
[27] See C. F. Keil and Franz Delitzsch, *Biblical Commentary on the Old Testament*, VIII, 88.

observed that this curse was fulfilled in three instances. Antiochus Epiphanes desecrated the temple during the Maccabean period, and Herod the Great altered it with a view to glorifying himself. Both of these men were smitten by a sudden awful disease and perished in great agony. The temple was destroyed by the Romans in A.D. 70, and later their own empire came to destruction.[28]

The result of Darius' decree is in verses 13-15. Governor Tatnai and his associates, either through an honest desire to perform the king's will or through a fear of his threat, "did speedily" what he had commanded. Of the Jews themselves it is said that they "builded"—the elders supervising the work and the younger men actually accomplishing it. Considerable credit is given in the Scriptures to the ministry of Haggai and Zechariah as greatly expediting the construction. From their own books we can see that Haggai rebuked and reproved, while Zechariah encouraged the people.[29] He did this by assuring them that God was with them, as well as by prophesying the future glory of the nation. Both types of ministry are just as necessary to the well-being of God's people today as they were in this Old Testament period.

It is stated that this labor was performed because "the God of Israel" commanded it (v. 13). To do His will is the one supremely important thing in life (see Heb. 13:20-21). Although He is of course "the God of heaven," yet He is also "the God of Israel."

The work was also done according to the commandment of Cyrus, Darius and Artaxerxes (v. 14b). The last-mentioned name provides a bit of a problem; the only Arta-

---

[28] See Ironside, p. 55; and Gaebelein, p. 23.
[29] See Luck, *The Bible* . . ., p. 149.

xerxes thus far mentioned is said to have hindered the work rather than to have commanded that it be done (chap. 4). But the Artaxerxes of chapter 7 did not reign until after the temple was completed. However, it seems more satisfactory to apply this statement to him, since it is explicitly stated that he commanded them to "beautify" the house of God (7:20, 27). Doubtless Ezra thought of this as being a part of "finishing" the temple and so brought in Artaxerxes' name in this connection.

The edifice was finally completed in the third day of the month Adar, in the sixth year of Darius' reign (515 B.C.). Haggai states that they recommenced work on the twenty-fourth day of the sixth month, in the second year of Darius (Hag. 1:14-15). Since Adar was the twelfth month (see Esther 3:7), this means it took almost four and a half years to complete the building after the new start was made. The foundation had been laid in the second year of King Cyrus (537 B.C.). Thus the total time spent, from first start to final completion, was approximately twenty-two years.

The dedication of the second temple is related in verses 16-18. Doubtless, remembering the example of King Solomon, the people consecrated the new house of God at a special ceremony. As might be expected, this was an occasion of much joy. No tears, as were shed at the laying of the foundation, are mentioned. Probably the ancient men (who had seen the original temple, and so wept over the prospect of this less glorious one) were by this time deceased. Be that as it may, regret over the past was forgotten in joy over the present blessings. It is possible for us even now to be hindered in a proper appreciation and use of present blessings by thinking too much of that which is past.

With regard to this matter, the determination of the Apostle Paul should be an example to each of us: "This one thing I do, forgetting those things which are behind, and reaching forth unto those things which are before, I press toward the mark for the prize of the high calling of God in Christ Jesus" (Phil. 3:13-14).

Comparing this dedication with that of Solomon's temple, the sacrifices offered were few in number—100 bullocks, 200 rams, 400 lambs. Solomon on that occasion had presented as an oblation no less than 22,000 oxen and 120,000 sheep (I Kings 8:63). But it must be borne in mind that Solomon was even then an exceedingly wealthy monarch. These returned exiles, like King Solomon, brought offerings commensurate with their ability. This is the standard to which God expects all of us to adhere: "Upon the first day of the week let every one of you lay by him in store, as God hath prospered him" (I Cor. 16:2).

Not in the abundance of the sacrifices, but in another feature lay the most striking distinction between the dedication of the second temple and that of the first. Scripture records:

> Now when Solomon had made an end of praying, the fire came down from heaven, and consumed the burnt-offering and the sacrifices; and the glory of the LORD filled the house. And the priests could not enter into the house of the LORD, because the glory of the LORD had filled the LORD's house (II Chron. 7:1-2).

In Zerubbabel's temple the Shekinah was absent. But nevertheless a wonderful promise was made—that the glory of the second temple would be greater than that of the first (Hag. 2:9). This prophecy was in due time fulfilled when the Lord Jesus Christ was eventually manifested in this temple, for Herod's Temple was but a continuation in remodeled form of that of Zerubbabel. The New Testament Gospels tell us that the Lord frequently visited and taught in it.

Of particular significance were the twelve he goats which were offered (v. 17), directly stated to have been for the twelve tribes of Israel. This makes it plain that representatives of all these tribes were present and that the full nation was still viewed as consisting not of one or two but of twelve tribes. At this time of temple consecration, it is also recorded that the priests and Levites were fully established in their official duties, as prescribed in the Mosaic law.

Not long afterward there took place a memorable celebration of the Passover and the Feast of Unleavened Bread (vv. 19-21). The temple completion and dedication took place in the twelfth month. The following month was one of special solemnity and significance in the Jewish religious calendar. In this first month of the year came the blessed Passover, which spoke typically of salvation through the shed blood of Christ (I Cor. 5:7). On this occasion all the spiritual leaders—priests and Levites—were most careful to purify themselves ceremonially. It is a truth of perpetual importance that those who are leaders in the Lord's work should so walk as to be an example to the rest of the flock (I Peter 5:3). It is interesting to observe from verse 20 that for some time it evidently had been customary for the priests and Levites to kill the Passover lambs for the rest of the people, rather than for each household to slay its own as had originally been done in the land of Egypt.

Certain persons are spoken of in verse 21 as those who

"had separated themselves . . . from the filthiness of the heathen of the land." Expositors differ as to whether these were Gentile proselytes to Judaism or actual Jews who had corrupted themselves but had returned to a separated position.

According to the law of Moses, immediately after the Passover, for a week's duration, the Feast of Unleavened Bread was to be held. This was also observed by the people. The New Testament makes it clear that for us this celebration typifies the holy life that ought to follow the receiving of Christ as Saviour (see I Cor. 5:7-8).

It is inspiring to read this account of the way in which the Lord stirred up the hearts of the people and made it possible for them to gain a great spiritual victory. As He stirred, they responded to accomplish that which was His will. Then God "made them joyful" (v. 22). It is also said that He "turned the heart of the king of Assyria unto them." The reference is evidently to King Darius. Just why he is here given this particular title is not now known, though it is true that he ruled over what was once the Assyrian Empire.

2

EZRA LEADS THE SECOND RETURN FROM EXILE AND RESTORES THE PEOPLE TO THEIR SEPARATED POSITIONS (7:1–10:44)

A Second Remnant Prepares To Return Under Ezra's Leadership (7:1-28)

The opening words of this chapter (and division of the book) span a considerable length of time—"Now after these things." Following the completion of the temple (approximately 515 B.C.), Darius Hystaspes reigned about thirty years longer (until 485 B.C.). He was then succeeded by his son Xerxes who ruled for twenty years (485-465 B.C.). The latter is apparently King Ahasuerus in the book of Esther. Xerxes was eventually assassinated by the captain of his guards. His son Artaxerxes Longimanus succeeded his father and avenged his murder, his reign extending from 465-425 B.C. Since Ezra 7 begins with Artaxerxes Longimanus in his seventh year on the throne, it is clear that about fifty-seven years had elapsed since the events with which chapter 6 concluded.

During the interim secular history tells us that Xerxes had made a belligerent expedition into Greece but had finally met with disastrous defeat. The remainder of his days

were spent in indolent living.[1] During this time he married
Esther, and she was providentially enabled to defeat Ha-
man's wicked plot to murder all the Jews. While the details
are not known, it is evident that Artaxerxes Longimanus
was quite friendly with the Jews, perhaps due to the influence of Esther and Mordecai. This monarch granted many
favors to Ezra and had Nehemiah as his cup-bearer.

At the time when chapter 7 begins, the people in Judea
were obviously in a backslidden and despondent condition.
No further reference is made to Zerubbabel and Joshua,
the great leaders who had no doubt died in the time interval
between chapters 6 and 7. At just this crisis, Ezra, an outstanding personage among the Jews still residing in Babylon, had it laid upon his heart to lead another group back
to Jerusalem.

The chapter commences with a genealogy of Ezra. Like
other such lists in the Bible it is evidently abbreviated, listing some of the outstanding names in the family tree all the
way back to Aaron, the brother of Moses. Seraiah, as has
been previously shown, was high priest at the time Jerusalem
fell to Nebuchadnezzar. The high priest Joshua was his
grandson. Since chapter 7 occurs some fifty years after
Joshua's time, Ezra must have been either the great-grand-
son or great-great-grandson of Seraiah. Between Azariah
and Meraioth (v. 3) six names are omitted which are recorded in I Chronicles 6:7-10. This should not be thought

[1] "Xerxes (486-465 B.C.), the son of Darius I the Great is undoubtedly the Ahasuerus of the book of Esther. The third year of his reign in which he held a great feast and assembly at Shushan (Susa), the palace, corresponds identically to the third year of the reign of Xerxes when he arranged the Grecian war. In the seventh year of his reign Xerxes returned defeated from Greece and consoled himself in the pleasures of his palace. It was then that Ahasuerus sought 'fair young virgins' and replaced Vashti by marrying Esther. An important historical inscription of Xerxes discovered at Persepolis lists the numerous subject nations over which he ruled, and fully corroborates Esther 1:1 that he ruled 'from India to Ethiopia.' " (Merrill F. Unger, *Unger's Bible Dictionary*, p. 31)

an oddity because, by comparison with Old Testament records, it can easily be seen that several names are omitted in the Messianic genealogy of Matthew 1. Clearly it was customary with the Jews to omit some of the names when preparing genealogical tables.

A considerable amount of information is given by Ezra as to himself and the part he played under God in this second return to Judea. His home had been in Babylon and he was a "ready scribe in the law" (v. 6). This is of especial interest since he is the first in the Bible to be called a scribe. "Ready" indicates that he was particularly skillful in his work. There is also here a strong testimony to the truth that the law of Moses was not a mere human code. It is called the law "which the LORD God of Israel had given."

Obviously Ezra was acquainted with the king and possessed his favor, for it is said that "the king granted him all his request." The details of this request are not stated, but valid conclusions as to its nature can be drawn from the statement of what the king did for him. In it all Ezra saw "the hand of the LORD his God upon him." Oh, that we might be quicker to see the hand of the Lord working in our own lives! "Every good gift and every perfect gift is from above, and cometh down from the Father of lights" (James 1:17a).

Before giving the details of the return to Jerusalem which he led, Ezra briefly summarizes the principal facts with the dates (vv. 7-10). In the returning party five groups are mentioned, similar to those in the first return of chapter 2. The journey took place in Artaxerxes' seventh year (458 B.C.), almost seventy years after the first return under Zerubbabel.

The trip began on the first day of the first month, which

was doubtless selected as an auspicious date—the beginning of the new year. The party arrived at Jerusalem exactly four months later. Some critics have claimed that this was an unreasonably long time for the journey involved. But it must be remembered that the group consisted not only of men, women and children, but that these people also were transporting household goods. Then too there were dangers and perils along the way, of which we know little today. When these and other factors are considered, the time spent in traveling does not seem at all out of proportion.

Verse 10 is one of the great verses of the book—indeed, of the whole Bible! "For Ezra had prepared his heart to seek the law of the LORD, and to do it, and to teach in Israel statutes and judgments." Here is the underlying secret of Ezra's successful life and ministry. He began not by preparing his head but by preparing his heart! Daniel began his successful life by purposing in his heart (Dan. 1:8), Ezra by preparing his heart. This simply means that he inwardly determined to make the three things specified the chief objective of his life. The first was to seek the law of the Lord, in other words, to study, to learn and to become familiar with God's law. His second goal was to do it—to put into practice in his own personal life the teachings of God's Word. His third purpose was to teach in Israel statutes and judgments. This means to go to others and teach them the Word of the Lord. It was Israel's disobedience to these statutes and judgments which had previously brought about the national downfall. Ezra had a noble determination to do his part to see that such a downfall would never again be the lot of the chosen people.

Artaxerxes' letter to Ezra (vv. 11-26) is another most unusual decree, demonstrating once more the power of God to work even in the hearts of heathen kings for the benefit of His servants. This is not a proclamation of a general nature such as that issued by Cyrus and recorded in chapter 1. This is rather a letter of authority granted to one specific person. It bestows upon Ezra quite a number of extraordinary powers and, at the same time, specifies certain ordinances which were to extend beyond even Ezra's lifetime.

In the letter Ezra is called a priest (v. 11), but the emphasis is laid on his work in the office of scribe. It is also significant to observe that the stress is laid not on the scribe's task of copying the law but on that of studying and teaching it. He was "a scribe of the words of the commandments of the LORD, and of his statutes to Israel." Compare this with the title Artaxerxes claimed for himself—"king of kings" (v. 12). This title was literally true for he did indeed rule over lesser, tributary kings. But of the two titles—that given to Ezra and that to Artaxerxes—is not Ezra's far grander? And today, although thousands of years have elapsed, Ezra's life is well known to many persons and continues to be a wonderful spiritual example. On the other hand, the great King Artaxerxes, were it not for the writing of this particular letter, would be practically forgotten.

Once again, as in the decrees of Cyrus and Darius, it is evident that this king also recognized Jehovah at least as being the supreme God, "the God of heaven." Artaxerxes then proceeded to confer power upon Ezra to take with him to Jerusalem all "the people of Israel" (this would include members of all the twelve tribes) who wished to return in a second great migration to Judea. Special mention was made of priests and Levites who might wish to return.

It was said of Ezra himself that he was "sent of the king." The "seven counsellors" of the king (v. 14) were probably members of the same group referred to in Esther 1:14, a cabinet composed of princes of the realm.

I was stipulated that Ezra was "to inquire concerning Judah and Jerusalem, according to the law of thy God which is in thy hand" (v. 14, ASV). This hardly means that he was to ascertain whether his people were keeping the law of God, for the king would not have been concerned as to that. It must then signify that he was to inquire as to the manner in which they were getting on, in other words, whether they were prospering.

Permission was granted to Ezra to receive gifts both of silver and of gold as an offering to God to be used in His house at Jerusalem. With these funds he was commanded to buy animals, as well as other items ordinarily used in the offerings, and to sacrifice them at the temple. The number to be purchased and used in this manner was left entirely to his discretion. Any balance of money which was left Ezra was empowered to use as he pleased in the service of God, "after the will of your God" (v. 18). It is later indicated (v. 27) that he understood this to refer to beautifying the temple.

Certain vessels were given to the godly scribe for service in the temple ministry. Those originally captured by Nebuchadnezzar had previously been restored by King Cyrus, so these must have been additional pieces of equipment needed on such special occasions as the annual feasts.

Anything beyond that already mentioned, which Ezra found was needed to put the temple in good shape, he was empowered to draw from the king's treasure house. An

order was given to all the treasurers on the west side of the
Euphrates that they should give Ezra whatever he desired
for such a purpose, up to one hundred talents of silver,[2]
one hundred measures of wheat, one hundred baths of wine,
one hundred baths of oil, and any quantity of salt he wanted. Though the relationship of Ezra to the king prior to
this time is not revealed, it is quite evident that the monarch
had unusual confidence in him. Tribute was collected from
the people of that day not only in money but also in produce, the best of such items being deposited in the king's
own treasury.

It was the king's command that anything Ezra felt to be
the will of God was to be done. His reason for such a strong
order is explained in the words "For why should there be
wrath against the realm of the king and his sons?" (v. 23b).
Clearly Artaxerxes was anxious not to displease Jehovah
God in any way, lest His wrath should fall on him and his
family. Secular history indicates that several years before
this present letter was written, Egypt, with the aid of
Athens, had successfully revolted against Persian rule.
About the same time that Artaxerxes sent Ezra to Jerusalem, he also sent out an expeditionary force to bring the
Egyptians back under his control. This campaign was suc-
cessful.

> Without pretending to penetrate the Divine counsels, it
> may be noticed that from the year B.C. 458, things went
> well for the Persians in Egypt. Memphis was recovered in
> that year or the next; and in B.C. 455 the Athenians were
> finally defeated, and the province recovered.[3]

[2] At the price silver sold for in the 1960's, this amount would be worth over $200,000 in
United States currency.
[3] *Pulpit Commentary*, VII, 111.

How many living sons Artaxerxes possessed at the time he mentioned them in his letter to Ezra is not known. History records that at his death he left behind him no less than eighteen.

The stipulation of verse 24 is of utmost importance. Not only the priests, but all of those who had anything to do with the temple ministry—Levites, singers, porters, Nethinims, miscellaneous workers—were to be exempted from taxation. Even today it is customary in many nations for strictly religious work to be tax exempt. As far as is now known, this temple exemption continued so long as Persia retained its control over Jerusalem.

In addition to the above mentioned favors, Ezra himself was given authority to govern his people, not only in Jerusalem but also "all the people that are beyond the river" (v. 25), the allusion being of course to the Euphrates. That this terminology referred to the Jews is made clear in that they are specified to be "all such as know the laws of thy God." Over the Jews in this large area, Ezra was granted power to set magistrates and judges. As for the Gentiles who dwelt around the Jews, Ezra was given the right to teach them the laws of God—"teach ye them that know them not."

The king's decree was not without what we today call "teeth." Upon Ezra was bestowed the authority to punish those under his control who disobeyed either the law of Jehovah ("thy God") or the Persian law. The type of punishment permitted is also specified—banishment and confiscation of goods, imprisonment, even death itself (v. 26).

Appended to this extraordinary decree of the king is Ezra's thanksgiving to God (vv. 27-28), a little hymn of praise to the Lord for the events He had brought to pass.

It is clear that Ezra himself had suggested this whole project to the king (see v. 6). Because the king had a high regard for this man of God, as well as implicit confidence in him, a most favorable response had been given. But Ezra does not give the credit to man, but to the One who "put such a thing as this in the king's heart." In the final analysis it was God who "extended mercy" to Ezra in the sight of the king and of his powerful nobles. This made the scribe sure that it was "the hand of the LORD" (v. 28) which was upon him, strengthening him for a great spiritual ministry. In such a confidence he gathered other chief men of Israel to go up to Jerusalem with him in this second momentous return. The trip having already been summarized (7:7-9), Ezra proceeded to describe it and its perils in detail in chapter 8.

The Journey of Ezra and His Company; Their Eventual Arrival in Jerusalem (8:1-36)

The record of the journey opened with the list of those who accompanied Ezra in this migration (vv. 1-14). As in the record of the first group which returned under Zerubbabel's leadership, the people were listed by families. Most of these families were also named in chapter 2. The chief differences between the two tabulations are that the second return took in fewer families than the first, and a lesser number of people. Those returning with Ezra totaled 1,514, including 1,496 people plus 18 heads of families. However, it is stated that this number included only adult males, so with women and children added probably the grand total was six or seven thousand. Although a sizeable number of souls for such a long overland trip, this is nothing like the number that came back with Zerubbabel.

However, it is not hard to understand the reasons for the greater size of the first returning group. There is a strong adventurous appeal to the idea of being for the first time released from captivity and going back to an almost unknown motherland to do strictly pioneer work. But when Ezra made his journey, the project was no longer novel because there had been Jews in Palestine for many years. And in addition the work in Judea was in a depressed and discouraging condition. These factors certainly made the romantic appeal practically nil.

It is recorded that a special gathering of the returning company was held at the river of Ahava (vv. 15-20). The returnees left this location on the twelfth day of the first month (v. 31). It has previously been stated that they left Babylon on the first day of the first month (7:9). Since they stayed at Ahava three days (v. 15), it is evident that it took them approximately nine days to reach that place from Babylon. The exact location of Ahava is at present unknown. Since it was obviously not far from Babylon, the river was probably a tributary of the mighty Euphrates, the latter of course running through the city of Babylon. Since so large a group could not be cared for in town, the company dwelt in tents while at Ahava.

Ezra chose this particular time for a close inspection of the returnees. He was shocked to find that no Levites were in the number (very few of them had returned with Zerubbabel, see 2:40). He therefore sent several of the leading men to Iddo, who was "chief at the place Casiphia" (v. 17). The location of Casiphia is also now unknown, but it is clear that many of the Levites dwelt there. Iddo, though one of the Nethinims rather than a Levite, was the chief man of the place. So to Iddo was sent a request: "Bring unto us ministers for the house of our God." Again a favorable answer came to Ezra's petition, and once more he ascribed it all to the goodness of God—"by the good hand of our God upon us" (v. 18a). Some forty of the Levites responded and no less than two hundred and twenty of the Nethinims. Ezra states that he possessed the names of each of these, but did not undertake to record them in his book (v. 20b).

Before the journey was commenced in earnest, Ezra called the people to a day of fasting and prayer (vv. 21-23). Special petition was made to God for a "right way"— a safe trip with no mishap. Evidently Ezra had originally used very strong terms in telling the king that the Lord Jehovah was a great and powerful God who would surely protect those who trusted Him and that He would bring trouble on those who forsook Him and His law. Now with the journey immediately before them, he began to realize very keenly the dangers and pitfalls they would face. They might have to deal with "the enemy in the way" (v. 22). The name or nature of this enemy is not specified, but the reference could be to marauding tribes of Arabs, or to miscellaneous robbers and plunderers. If such heard of the treasure carried by the returnees, they might well lie in wait for them. Ezra had a strong feeling that the king who had granted so many other favors would also give them an escort of soldiers for protection. But after boasting to Artaxerxes of the greatness of his God and of His ever present care of His own, Ezra was now ashamed to ask for human guardians.

He did not, however, set out in a presumptuous and self-confident way. Instead he and the people entreated the Lord in prayer until they were sure they had from Him the answer to their request. It remains only to be added that God did indeed protect them from harm on the way.

Before finally leaving, however, one other item remained to be cared for. Twelve of the leading priests had the treasure for the temple committed to them (vv. 24-30). This whole matter was handled in a most businesslike way (in New Testament times the Apostle Paul exerted similar care in sending to Jerusalem the offering for the poor saints there, II Cor. 8:16-21). The money, being in bullion, had to be weighed out. The silver and gold vessels were likewise weighed. The priests in whose charge these valuables were placed had an earnest exhortation given them by Ezra, who reminded them that they were holy men of God and that this silver and gold was in like manner holy to the Lord. This message was intended to encourage them to be perfectly honest in their dealings, lest any might be tempted to purloin something for himself, even as Achan of old had stolen that which was devoted to God (Joshua 7). It is difficult to determine the exact value of these treasures in terms of modern-day currency, but at present prices the silver would have been valued in the hundreds of thousands of dollars, and the gold in the millions. This helps to understand the great concern Ezra felt over the perils of the way. Even at the present time to transport such a sum through the streets of one of our cities would require a strong guard of men with an armored car.

The four-month journey is covered in verse 31. Without giving details the statement seems to hint at narrow escapes "from the hand of the enemy" and from "such as lay in wait by the way." But God's hand was long enough to reach and protect His servants all the journey long. Verses 32-36 tell of the arrival at Jerusalem and the first things done after reaching there. Evidently three days passed without activity. Doubtless during this time the people were resting from their arduous trip and rendering thanks to God for His merciful care.

On the fourth day the priests who had the responsibility of the gold, silver and vessels transferred these things to the temple authorities. All was done "decently and in order" (I Cor. 14:40). The gold and silver were weighed, and the vessels were both counted and weighed. A large treasure had been placed in the hands of these priests, and they handled it very faithfully. Christians today have also in their possession a veritable treasure—"the *faith* which was once delivered unto the saints" (Jude 3*b*). This we must be prepared to defend earnestly for one day we too must make an accounting (II Cor. 5:10). God grant that each of us will then be able to hear the voice of our Lord saying, "Well done, thou good and faithful servant" (Matt. 25:21).

At this time also the returnees offered sacrifices to God. These were similar to the ones presented by Zerubbabel's party but lesser in number to correspond to the smaller size of the group. Ezra and his assistants in addition notified all the Persian officials of the king's royal decree, with the powers and rights it conferred on the scribe and his people. The result was that these authorities "furthered the people, and the house of God." This means that they provided no opposition but instead aided the Israelites, supplying the things for their temple service which the king had stipulated.

Ezra Finds the People Have Lost Their Separated Position (9:1-4)

The chapter's opening phrase "Now when these things were done" points to the passage of a period of time during which the various officials were informed of Ezra's authority and responded by helping forward the work. Weeks or even months may have been involved. It has already been stated that Ezra reached Jerusalem the first day of the fifth month. The next date cited (10:9) is the twentieth day of the ninth month.

After Ezra had been in the land for a while, he was informed of a serious failure on the part of the people who resided there (vv. 1-2). It was not the religious leaders who brought this information to him, but the civil authorities—the princes. Apparently from the time of Zerubbabel's decease to the coming of Ezra, the governing of the people was in the hands of a group of princes rather than one man.

The complaint made was of a grievous lack of separation on the part of the people in general, and even of the priests and Levites who should have been the spiritual leaders. In disobedience to the command of God (Deut. 7:1-6), the men of the land had married heathen wives, women from the remnants of the Canaanites as well as from various surrounding nations—Ammon, Moab, Egypt. The people of Israel were "the holy seed" (v. 2) who had been chosen by God and set apart to be a people for His name. But sad to say, the holy seed had mixed with the wicked idolatrous people of the land. Failure of this very nature had once led astray even such a man of God as Solomon (I Kings 11:1-10). In such unions the offspring would naturally be inclin-

ed to follow the religion of the mother. If this had continued, in all too short a time Israel would have been swallowed
up by the godless heathen around them.

Ezra's informers made it plain that not merely the lower
class of Hebrews had done this. The leading figures had
been the very chief in this transgression of God's command.

The effect of this information upon Ezra was startling
(vv. 3-4). His feeling might well be compared with that of a
pious pilgrim visiting Rome at the time of its most shame-
less corruption. The place always considered the apex of
holiness would prove instead to be a veritable sewer of
corruption. Ezra's grief was indeed great, issuing in the
tearing of his clothing and pulling out his hair. The rending
of the clothes was a rather common Oriental way of mani-
festing deep sorrow and is mentioned frequently in the
Bible.[4] The plucking out of a portion of the hair by the
roots is by no means so common (cf. Isa. 22:12). Some
hold it to be an evidence of unusual grief, others of great
moral indignation.

After these outward manifestations, Ezra seated himself,
evidently for several hours, speechless with astonishment.
It astounded him to think that after all the troubles of
Israel and their subsequent restoration by God they should
once again start a downward course away from Him. As
he sat in silent amazement, there gathered around him a
crowd of like-minded people. These were earnest Israelites
who, like Ezra, "trembled at the words of the God of Israel."
They were filled with godly fear at the words the Lord had
spoken, telling of the awful judgment He would bring on

[4] See, e.g., Gen. 37:29, 34; Num. 14:6; Joshua 7:6; Judges 11:35; II Sam. 1:11; I Kings
21:27; Esther 4:1; Job 1:20; Joel 2:13.

His people when they were disobedient to His righteous commands.

Ezra Carries the Matter to God in a
Great Prayer of Confession (9:5-15)

The time of the evening sacrifice is said to have been about 3 p.m.[5] It seems that it had become a custom for people to gather at that time each day in one of the courts of the temple for the purpose of prayer. When the officiating priest had finished offering the sacrifice he would come forth and pronounce the benediction at this public gathering. It was at this particular time that Ezra offered his great prayer to the Lord. The sacrifice itself speaks of atonement (Lev. 17:11), the only means by which guilty sinners can have boldness to come into the presence of a holy God (Heb. 9:11-12; 10:19).

Again there was the outward manifestation of torn garment and mantle. Then Ezra knelt before God with hands outstretched to heaven as he prayed. The prayer itself is in its entirety one of confession of sin, with no petition or request of any kind. The man of God also perfectly identified himself with his people in his prayer, speaking of "our trespass," "we have forsaken thy commandments," etc. Obviously he himself was not personally guilty of these sins, but he spoke as the representative, the intercessor for his nation.

Ezra was not like certain ones of whom Jeremiah spoke —men who could recklessly sin and then show not the slightest shame, not even a blush (Jer. 6:15; 8:12). He was

---

[5] According to the Rabbis the lamb was slain at the eighth hour and a-half, or about 2:30 p.m., and the pieces laid on the altar an hour later—about 3:30 p.m." (Alfred Edersheim, *The Temple: Its Ministry and Services*, p. 144).

consumed with shame to think of the iniquity of his people (v 6.). He compared their sins with a flood that had risen till it covered them, indeed until it had "grown up unto the heavens" where God could not help but see and judge it. Ezra acknowledged that from earliest days Israel had been, so to speak, in one great trespass against the Lord (v. 7). Because of this disobedience and sinfulness, they had suffered fierce affliction and "confusion of face" down to the very time at which he was speaking.

In comparison with their earlier history, Ezra spoke of the time since they had been restored to their land as "a little space" (v. 8). Despite their ancestors' iniquity, the Lord had for this "little space" again shown them His grace, His unmerited favor. From the captivity itself, He had allowed "a remnant to escape." To this group He had given "a nail in his holy place." In Scripture metaphor the nail speaks of security and firmness (cf. Isa. 22:23). In the comparative simplicity of those days, large nails or spikes were often driven in walls to provide hangers for utensils and other items. So the thought expressed is that God had once again given them a secure place in the Holy Land. In addition to security, God had also lightened their eyes, which had to do with strengthening (see I Sam. 14:27).

Although they were no more than slaves in a strange land, the Lord had so wrought in their behalf as to give them favor with the kings of Persia, thus allowing the work to be revived, the temple to be rebuilt, and shelter to be provided for them (v. 9), (the wall mentioned does not refer to that of the city which had not yet been rebuilt).

But now, after having received all these mercies, they had once more forsaken God's commandments (v. 10).

What excuse could be offered? Ezra quoted Deuteronomy 7:3 and alluded to various other scriptures, all showing that God had directly commanded the Israelites not to intermarry with the wicked people of the land, but instead to remain separate. If they did this, He promised that they would "eat the good of the land," leaving it in due time for a possession to their children after them.

Ezra frankly acknowledged that all the horrible afflictions which had come upon the nation were really far less than they deserved (v. 13). From these trials God had been exceedingly gracious in granting deliverance. But now, if they once more break His commandments and corrupt themselves, what can they expect but that He will descend on them in total annihilation (v. 14)?

Ezra closed his fervent prayer by speaking of the righteousness of God (v. 15). Why should He not in justice consume them? They remained before Him but an escaped remnant caught, so to speak, in the very act of their wickedness. They could not stand before the Lord, for they had no excuse whatever for their deeds. The language is reminiscent of Psalm1:5: "Therefore the ungodly shall not stand in the judgment, nor sinners in the congregation of the righteous."

Revival Begins (10:1-8)

The opening verse relates the result of Ezra's prayer upon the people. As already seen, while he sat astonished for several hours, a considerable number of spiritually minded people had gathered about him. Now as he, a great man and their governor, prayed so fervently with such visible signs of overpowering emotion—"weeping and casting himself down"—the report spread quickly and a tremendous crowd soon assembled. The place of assemblage was "before the house of God," which means in the courts of the temple. The hearts of the throng were really touched and all began to weep "very sore."

H. A. Ironside comments that nothing like this would have happened if Ezra, when he heard of their sin, had drawn himself up in a pharisaical attitude and, coldly denouncing them, had withdrawn from the people altogether. He speaks of some today who do this very thing, calling them "spiritual Ishmaelites, their hand against every man, and every man's hand against them; criticizing, fault-finding, restless and unhappy; occupied with evil, lamenting the conditions of the times; bewailing the unfaithfulness of anybody and everybody but themselves; and so falling into a spirit of Pharisaism that is helpful to no one, and a hindrance to all they come in contact with. Now all this results from occupation with persons instead of with Christ."[6]

Occasionally at the present time we say or sing, "Lord, send a revival and let it begin in me." On this occasion a revival truly did begin in one man, Shechaniah, whose father was one of those guilty of the very sin Ezra had just condemned. This man spoke to Ezra acknowledging the transgression but suggesting a remedy (vv. 2-4). He suggested that all the people make a covenant with God to put away these heathen wives and children in accordance with the law (see Deut. 24:1). Ezra himself, as the governor, was asked to supervise this matter, while the people would support him. Then Shechaniah urged, "Arise . . . be of good courage."

[6] H. A. Ironside, *Notes on Ezra, Nehemiah and Esther*, pp. 82-83.

Parenthetically let it be said that under grace the procedure taught in such cases is quite the opposite of that stipulated under law. For proof of this, compare the Old Testament teaching with that given in I Corinthians 7:12-14, 16.

After having prayed, Ezra proceeded to act (vv.5-8). Shechaniah's encouragement and suggestion were accepted. Rising up, Ezra immediately made the priests, Levites and other Israelites present swear that they would do as Shechaniah had said. In addition a proclamation was sent throughout the whole city and province calling all the men of Israel to assemble themselves together at Jerusalem within three days to make the matter right with God. The farthest boundary at that time was no more than forty miles from Jerusalem, so it would be easily possible for all to gather within the prescribed time.[7]

In the meantime, Ezra himself continued his mourning in secret, fasting in the room of Johanan. Sometimes a fast consists of only abstaining from certain foods, and as a rule one is considered as fasting when he does not partake of any food, though he may still drink water. But Ezra's was an absolute fast from both food and drink.

> The man who sets himself to seek, to do, to teach the law of God invariably brings himself to where sorrow will be his portion and intrepid courage his only strength. If such devotion issue in such experiences, it also is the secret of strength, enabling a man to stand for God, and realize His purpose; and thus, moreover, to be the true friend and deliverer of the people of God.[8]

[7] *Pulpit Commentary*, VII, 153.
[8] G. Campbell Morgan, *An Exposition of the Whole Bible*, pp. 189-90.

As to Ezra's deep exercise of soul about this sin of his people, A. C. Gaebelein cogently comments:

> This is what is so sadly lacking in our own days. So many make light of the sin and worldliness of those who profess the Name of Christ, there is but little heart searching, true humiliation and self-judgment to be seen. Such is the spirit of Laodicea.[9]

A penalty was placed on failure to attend the announced assembly. The one who did not present himself would have all his possessions confiscated, while he himself would be banished from the land—excommunicated from the number of the people of Israel.

It is interesting to follow up the reference to Johanan (v. 6). According to Nehemiah 12:10-11, 22, Joshua the high priest was succeeded by his son Joiakim. Joiakim held the office in the interval between Ezra 6 and 7. Then the office fell to his son Eliashib (see Neh. 3:1). Johanan (or Jonathan) was the grandson of the latter. He rightfully possessed a room among the chambers connected with the temple, and this is where Ezra resorted during his fast.

THE PEOPLE RETURN TO THEIR
SEPARATED POSITION (10:9-44)

At the required time the Israelites assembled themselves in the "broad place before the house of God" (v. 9, ASV). The great court of the temple is evidently referred to here. An ancient authority states that this court was 500 by 150 feet in size. It has been estimated that such a space could accommodate 20,000 men.[10] Probably the number of able-bodied men at that period did not exceed this figure.

---

[9] A. C. Gaebelein, *The Annotated Bible*, III: *Ezra-Psalms*, 37.
[10] *Pulpit Commentary*, VII, 153.

The time was the ninth month (our December), the rainy season in that part of the world. Realizing that the affair had to do with matters which would mean the separation of many families, there was a trembling among all the people, partly from emotion and partly from the discomfort of a heavy rain.

Ezra spoke boldly to the whole group, advising them frankly that they had trespassed against the Lord. He exhorted them to confess to the Lord their sin and to put away their heathen wives. He also commanded them to "separate . . . from the people of the land" (v. 11). Heathen wives would naturally lead to fellowship and union with heathen in-laws.

Though doubtless many hearts ached, the congregation as a whole answered "with a loud voice," promising to do what Ezra had asked (v. 12). However, the suggestion was offered that since many people were involved and the weather was not propitious, a final settlement could not be made then and there. It was advised that the rulers of all the people, in connection with the elders of the various cities, examine each case individually during a reasonable period of time. Then everything could be properly cared for without unfortunate mistakes being made. It is clear that this proposition was not offered for the purpose of delaying settlement but rather to facilitate the matter so that all things might be done "decently and in order." The hearts of the people evidently were genuinely moved with a desire to have "the fierce wrath of our God . . . turned from us" (v. 14).

The translation given in the Authorized Version for verse 15 would make it apparently contradict verse 16, since it states that only four men were employed in this matter, whereas the latter verse says that Ezra and certain others did the judging. But in the American Standard Version verse 15 is rendered: "Only Jonathan . . . and Jahzeiah . . . stood up against this matter." It seems that they and the other two mentioned in the verse were the only ones who opposed the plan as it had been outlined in verses 12-14. The reason for their opposition is not given. Possibly they had heathen wives they did not want to put away. Or it could have been that they desired an immediate settling of the matter, and therefore were against putting it off to a future date. Regardless of the motive, their opinion did not prevail. The plan suggested by the people was put into effect.

During a three-month period, Ezra and the elders examined all suspected cases (vv. 16-17). Besides the Jerusalem leaders, the chief of each family group examined was present.

The final feature of Ezra's book is a list of the men who had taken "strange wives" (vv. 18-44). To have their names published in such a list was a punishment in itself for the offenders. Seventeen priests head the number (vv. 18-22). Of these, four were in the family of the high priest Joshua. Next came ten Levites (vv. 23-24). Since the priests and Levites were the religious leaders it was fitting that they be listed separately.

The names of the balance of the culprits follow (vv. 25-43). The 86 listed, with the priests and Levites, totaled 113. This number at first thought hardly seems as large as might be expected. But the matter was nevertheless serious because it represented a rapidly increasing trend. Another side of the question which further thought reveals is this: the condition was alarming because almost 25 percent of the total number of offenders were religious leaders. "A little leaven leaveneth the whole lump" (I Cor. 5:6; Gal. 5:9).

The closing verse again affirms that the entire list given had married heathen wives. In addition, in certain of the cases there were offspring. This would of course make the separation more difficult. It is very likely that this "divorce court" also saw to it that suitable material support was provided for the families which had to be put away.

With this picture the account of Ezra concludes. The book as a whole has recorded real spiritual advances on the part of the people of God. The temple had been rebuilt. The province had received a good governor in Ezra. Spiritual revival had come to the people as they realized anew the importance of God's children living separated lives.

NEHEMIAH

OUTLINE

1. Nehemiah Returns to Jerusalem and Rebuilds the Walls (1:1—6:19)

   Nehemiah Learns of the Afflictions of the Remnant and Jerusalem (1:1-11)

   Nehemiah Is Sent to Jerusalem and Makes His Plans There (2:1-20)

   The Remnant Builds the Wall (3:1-32)

   The Work Continues Despite Opposition (4:1-23)
      1. Opposition by Ridicule (4:1-6)
      2. Opposition by Threat of Open Attack (4:7-9)
      3. Opposition from Discouragement (4:10)
      4. Opposition from Threat of Secret Attack (4:11-23)

   The Work Is Hindered by Selfishness and Greed (5:1-19)

   The Wall Is Completed (6:1-19)

2. Spiritual Revival Breaks Out (7:1—10:39)

   Nehemiah Makes Provision for Rule in Jerusalem (7:1-4)

   Nehemiah Prepares to Take a Census and Finds the Register of Those Who Returned with Zerubbabel (7:5-73)

   Ezra Teaches the Law (8:1-12)

   The Feast of Tabernacles Is Observed (8:13-18)

   Revival Comes (9:1-38)

   A Covenant Is Made To Be Faithful to God (10:1-39)

3. FURTHER REFORMS DEVELOP (11:1—13:31)

Provision Made for the Repopulation of Jerusalem (11:1-36)

Important Lists (12:1-26)

The Dedication of the Wall (12:27-47)

Nehemiah's Return to Jerusalem and His Correction of Disorders There (13:1-31)

BACKGROUND

AUTHORSHIP

It is plainly stated in the opening verse that Nehemiah was the human author of this book. Sometimes he speaks of himself in the third person, as did Ezra. This was a common practice of authors in the past and almost to the present day. Nehemiah's name means "Jehovah comforts." His father was Hachaliah ("Jehovah is hidden"). He had a brother named Hanani (1:2; 7:2). Beyond this nothing is known of his family, not even from which of the twelve tribes he came. It is clear that he was born in captivity and somehow rose to the position of cupbearer of King Artaxerxes Longimanus (1:11; 2:1), the same monarch referred to in Ezra 7:1. At Nehemiah's request, the king made him governor of Judah, which position he apparently held for about twelve years (5:14; 8:9; 10:1). As to his subsequent life and death following this period, the Bible is silent.

DATE

A comparison of Ezra 7:8 and Nehemiah 1:1; 2:1 will show that the events of Nehemiah's record began approximately twelve years after the closing scene in Ezra. The narrative of the book of Nehemiah covers another twelve-year period (cf. 2:1; 5:14; 13:6). The history here recorded occurred approximately 445-433 B.C.

Purpose

As in the book of Ezra, the author of this book presents a plain, straightforward account of a most important period of Jewish history. By the time that twelve years had passed after the revival with which Ezra closes, the people of Judah had again declined to an extremely depressing condition. Although they had by now dwelt in their land for almost a century since Zerubbabel returned and had long since completed the temple structure, they were still harassed by their enemies. Never had they been able to rebuild the walls of Jerusalem, a very necessary protection in that day and time (1:3). Although Ezra was still present with them, they were "in great affliction and reproach."

Securing the appointment of governor, Nehemiah came to them with official instructions to rebuild the city (2:5-6). Before that could actually be done, however, the walls had to be rebuilt (2:17). The book shows how this was accomplished and the people spiritually revived under the leadership of Nehemiah. The main theme is "Rebuilding the Walls of Jerusalem" see 1:3; 2:13, 15, 17; 4:6; 6:15; 12:27). The words "wall" and "walls" are used thirty-two times in the narrative, while "build" is used twenty-three times.

The book is of great significance today because it is filled with practical spiritual lessons, applicable to the people of God in any age as they seek to carry on His work. Especially is its message challenging in times of spiritual depression and discouragement.

1

NEHEMIAH RETURNS TO JERUSALEM AND REBUILDS THE WALLS (1:1–6:19)

Nehemiah Learns of the Afflictions of the Remnant and Jerusalem (1:1-11)

This is the only Bible book of history that begins with the name of the author as it is here given. Tradition says the Jews originally placed Ezra and Nehemiah together as one book. If so, this sentence was very likely written in order to show the exact point at which the change of human authorship took place.

The story opens in the month Chisleu, which is defined in Zechariah 7:1 as the ninth month. It corresponded to the latter part of November and the opening portion of December in our calendar. The year was the twentieth of the reign of Artaxerxes Longimanus.

Nehemiah first appears on the scene in the royal palace at Shushan. Shushan was called Susa by the Greeks and was the capital of the province of Elam. The name of the city means "lily" and is said to have been given because of the abundance of lilies that grew in the locality.[1] The monarchs of Persia maintained a winter residence there. Shushan

[1] Merrill F. Unger, *Unger's Bible Dictionary,* p. 1022.

also was the place where Daniel received his vision of the ram and goat (Dan. 8:2). Subsequent to Daniel's time, it was the home of Mordecai and Esther; in its palace Esther lived as queen.

The site of Shushan was excavated at the beginning of the twentieth century, and in 1901 the famous Code of Hammurabi was discovered there. Archaeologists have found that at the site "the most splendid monument of Persian Susa is the royal palace," started by Darius Hystaspes and completed by later kings. The outline of the palace can still be seen. The beautiful building was made of

> cedar wood from Lebanon, silver from Egypt, gold from Bactria, and ivory from India. . . . Panels of artistically colored glazed bricks constituted the most remarkable feature in the palace decorations. Many of the designs were executed in relief and show winged bulls and griffins, and include the famous "spearman of the guard." [2]

For some reason a group of Persian Jews had just visited Jerusalem, then had returned to Shushan. Included in their number was Nehemiah's brother Hanani. When he saw them, Nehemiah asked the travelers regarding "the Jews that had escaped, which were left of the captivity," meaning the remnant that had returned to the land of Judah, in contrast with those who had remained in foreign countries. It was clear that Nehemiah knew a number had returned and were living once more in the land. However, he had no recent information as to how they were prospering.

The answer he received (v. 3) was a sad one. The people of Judah, he learned, were "in great affliction and re-

[2] *Ibid.*, p. 1023.

proach." It was difficult for them to get by, facing as they did the reproach of various enemies and adversaries. The root of their trouble at Jerusalem was the exceedingly dilapidated condition of the walls and gates of the city. Some commentators argue that this statement could not refer to the ruinous condition of the walls dating back to the time of Nebuchadnezzar's conquest, so they imagine that the walls had later been rebuilt and then broken down once more just before the beginning of Nehemiah's book. But there is no record in Ezra or elsewhere of such a rebuilding of the walls. It seems very clear that although the remnant had finally reconstructed the temple and certain portions of the city, they had never been able to restore the walls of Jerusalem. Some attempt may have been started to accomplish this work but, if so, it had been unsuccessful. Until such a wall was absolutely completed, it would be of practically no value whatever. It is hard to understand just how essential a city wall was in ancient times. It was an indispensable protection both against the attacks of the armed forces of enemy communities and against depredations of robber bands, especially at night.

The news produced a striking reaction in Nehemiah, a reaction that brought him to his knees in prayer (vv. 4-11). Apparently he had little knowledge before of actual conditions at Jerusalem. Also, perhaps the situation became more graphic to him as seen through the eyes of his own brother. Whatever the cause, the tragic condition of the city now struck him with great force. Although he personally had a high position in Persia and was greatly prospering, yet it grieved him deeply to learn that the Lord's work, which centered in Jerusalem and the temple, was in a depressed state. This provides a sad contrast to many Christians of today who show little concern for the Lord's work as long as they themselves prosper materially.

Nehemiah's first action after he received the bad news was to sit down and weep.[3] Then for an extended period, "certain days," he mourned, fasted and prayed. After this he presented his special petition to the Lord. Most of the chapter is occupied with this prayer, one of the greatest in the Bible. The many allusions to previous writings of the Old Testament verify the fact that Nehemiah, besides being a man of prayer, was also a student of God's Word.

Nehemiah's prayer is directed to God as the all-powerful One who is ever merciful to His people. He prayed as one who knew the Lord, calling himself His "servant," as one who had uttered many prayers previously ("day and night"). He confessed the sins of Israel, saying, "We have sinned against thee." In this he deliberately and specifically included himself and his own personal ancestors. All had added their portion to the total transgression of the nation, which had resulted in this judgment of God. Nehemiah acknowledged that he and his people had broken God's holy laws as given through Moses. Therefore they well deserved all the trouble the Lord had allowed to come upon them.

But then Nehemiah reminded the Lord of His gracious promise, also given through Moses, that if after transgres-

---

[3] It may surprise some in our part of the world to read of strong men, such as Nehemiah and Ezra, weeping, as our culture has propagated for a long time the idea that tears, especially in a male, are a sign of weakness and thus "unmanly." Oriental culture has apparently had no such inhibition. "Eastern peoples show none of the restraint of emotion in lamentation which is characteristic of modern Occidentals, and there are many records of this manifestation of woe, even among men accustomed to hardships and warfare, such as David and his soldiers." In the instances recorded in Scripture weeping is more frequently associated with mental distress than with physical pain (*International Standard Bible Encyclopedia*, V, 2923). Scripture records the weeping of many of its chief male characters, including Abraham, Esau, Jacob, Benjamin, Joseph, Saul, David, Hezekiah, Job, Peter, Paul and John. The most manly Man who ever lived on this earth also wept (John 11:35; Luke 19:41; Heb. 5:7).

sion and divine scattering among the nations they turned back to Him and kept His commandments, then He would regather and restore them to Jerusalem, "the place that I have chosen to set my name there" (v.9). These statements of Nehemiah summarize the teaching of several passages in the Pentateuch, such as Deuteronomy 28:63-67; 30:1-5.

At first thought it may seem that these passages were not very appropriate to the situation then existing, as God had already in a measure fulfilled such promises. The people had already been regathered and brought back to their land. But the thought of Nehemiah evidently was that God had not completely fulfilled His word. Did not the promise imply that when He did bring them back He would not do so merely to allow them to be further afflicted and reproached, but would establish and bless them in the land? To the Lord, Nehemiah said, "Now *these are* thy servants" (v. 10). They had endured much hardship and sacrifice to return to the Holy Land and rebuild the temple. They were God's servants whom He had redeemed and brought back to their home country, even as He had once redeemed their ancestors from Egypt.

At the close of his prayer, Nehemiah brought his petition to the Lord. No doubt the resolve had already arisen in his mind to go himself to Jerusalem to assist in the work there, but to do this he needed special permission from the king. So he prayed that the Lord would "grant him mercy in the sight of this man," meaning Artaxerxes.

After the prayer, the one additional sentence with which the chapter closes makes clear the reason why Nehemiah needed the king's direct assent—he was cupbearer to Artaxerxes. Authorities state that in ancient times this official tasted food and wine and then passed it to the people at the king's table.[4] He was chosen for his handsome appearance and was a person of noble birth and rank. Usually he possessed considerable influence with the king, being often near him. In Bible history the cupbearer of Pharaoh was instrumental in bringing Joseph before the king of Egypt (Gen. 40-41).

Nehemiah Is Sent to Jerusalem and Makes His Plans There (2:1-20)

About four months later Nehemiah's request was granted by the king (vv. 1-8). During all this time the cupbearer had not mentioned his idea to the ruler, nor had he shown any grief in the monarch's presence. It may be that for most of the period the king had been at his winter residence. Finally Nehemiah in carrying out his duties was no longer able to conceal his depression of spirit. The king observed and commented on the fact that Nehemiah was evidently sad. Since he obviously was in good bodily health, the ruler rightly concluded that the sorrow must come from a condition of the heart rather than the body.

Although the king's question seemed kind, Nehemiah confesses that he was afraid. According to the court etiquette of the day it was considered highly improper for a subject to appear before the ruler in a sorrowful condition (cf. Esther 4:2). The monarchs of Persia operated on the theory that merely to be in the king's presence and enjoy his favor was sufficient to give perfect joy and happiness to the heart of any man. In addition to this, Nehemiah had in mind to request permission to go to Jerusalem. This too

---

[4] See Unger, p. 230.

would be utterly contrary to royal etiquette of the day—it would be an unheard of thing for one enjoying the king's august presence and favor to ask leave to depart to another place!

In spite of his fear, however, Nehemiah spoke both frankly and courageously. "Let the king live for ever" was a set phrase of the day, more or less like the more recent "Long live the king." After saying this, Nehemiah suggested to the king that he could not help but be sad when the city in which were located the tombs of his ancestors was wasted and ruined. This makes it clear that the family of Nehemiah had formerly dwelt at Jerusalem. It is said that the rulers of Persia had great respect for the graves of their ancestors, thus Nehemiah's question would be well inclined to strike a responsive chord in Artaxerxes.

Secular historians have characterized Artaxerxes Longimanus as the mildest and most magnanimous of all Persian monarchs. In this interview with Nehemiah he certainly acted in accordance with this reputation. Immediately sensing that Nehemiah had a desire to express to him concerning the situation at Jerusalem, he invited his cupbearer to make his request. In the moment or two which elapsed between the king's question and Nehemiah's answer, the latter silently uttered a prayer to God. This is another evidence that prayers do not have to be lengthy in order to be "effectual" and "fervent" (cf. James 5:16).

The petition Nehemiah made to Artaxerxes was that he be sent to Judah for the purpose of building the city of Jerusalem. Many who profess to be God's children seem to prefer to tear down rather than to build. In a sense it is easier for one possessing just a little discernment to tear down—to criticize—what others are doing than to build in a constructive way. But as servants of the Lord our chief task is to build (II Cor. 10:8), to build up our own lives in the faith (I Peter 2:2) and to build up ("edify") others (I Thess. 5:11). Of course it is sometimes necessary to tear down a worthless old structure before a new and worthwhile one can be built.

Intimating that he was willing to grant his cupbearer's request, the king asked certain questions as to how long the journey would take and the date when Nehemiah expected to return. This confirms the high regard the king bore for him, for he was anxious to have him back. Nehemiah set a definite time which is not specified here. It is later revealed that he served as governor for twelve years (5:14). However, it is unlikely that he mentioned such a long period in this first conversation with the king. Probably a shorter time was stipulated in the beginning, with an extension being granted later.

Nehemiah especially comments on the fact that this permission from the king was granted him in the presence of the queen. History indicates that the queens of Persia did not take part in state councils with their husbands. However, it should be remembered that this was not an official time of business but rather during a meal. Plutarch writes that Artaxerxes married his sister Amytis.[5] Ctesias, a Greek physician who later served in the Persian court, says that his wife was named Damaspia.[6] However, nothing is known about the latter except that she died on the same day as did her husband. Whether the queen of whom Nehemiah writes was one of these or still another woman is not known.

[5] *Encyclopedia Britannica*, 11th ed., II, 661.
[6] *Pulpit Commentary*, VII, 10.

Special request was made by Nehemiah to the king for letters of safe conduct to the various governors west of the Euphrates, so that he might obtain their assistance on his journey. The portion of the empire located east of the Euphrates, being nearer to the center of authority, was doubtless safer for travel.

In addition Nehemiah asked for a letter to Asaph, the keeper of the king's forest. While the exact location of this royal forest preserve is not known, evidently it was near Jerusalem. From it Nehemiah wished to obtain timber to use in repairing "the palace which appertained to the house" (v. 8) of God, the temple. The building he had in mind apparently was the fortress situated just northwest of the temple, which overlooked and protected the temple area itself. Herod the Great later rebuilt this fortress and named it for his friend Mark Anthony, calling it the Tower of Antonia. The most important event that ever took place there was the appearance of the Lord Jesus Christ before Pontius Pilate, who made the Tower of Antonia his headquarters while in Jerusalem. Still later the Apostle Paul spoke from its steps to the multitude just after his arrest.

Nehemiah also wanted materials for the wall of the city, as well as for his own residence ("the house that I shall enter into"). While not explicitly stated, it was evidently understood that Nehemiah was to act as governor during his sojourn at Jerusalem. Previous governors had possessed no official residence.

His request in its entirety was graciously granted by the ruler. Just as Ezra had done earlier, Nehemiah viewed this blessing as coming directly from God, saying that the king acted "according to the good hand of my God upon me."

The journey to Jerusalem is covered in few words (vv. 9-11). En route Nehemiah delivered to the different officials west of the Euphrates the epistles from the king which showed his own authority and purpose. He had a party of soldiers accompanying him, and it is evident that the trip was made much more rapidly than it had been by Ezra's group.

Verse 10 contains the first reference to Sanballat the Horonite who evidently was the governor of Samaria. Horonite is thought by some to be derived from the name of a town in Moab. However, this hardly seems reasonable, for then would he not have been called a Moabite as was Ruth? One commentary [7] traces the term to Beth-horon, a town in Ephraim, but in Nehemiah's day in the possession of the Samaritans. Tobiah the Ammonite, called "the servant," seems clearly to have been the servant of Sanballat, probably serving as his secretary and confidential adviser. When the letters from Artaxerxes were delivered, one of them came to Sanballat and Tobiah who were much displeased by its contents. Before this time the Samaritans had been filled with hatred at the sight of the returning Jews and had done their best to disrupt the work. Between these two capitals so near each other—Jerusalem and Samaria—the hostility was sharp. This feeling of enmity continued even down into New Testament days (cf. John 4:9 and the parable of the good Samaritan). Sanballat and his crowd did not want Jerusalem to prosper, therefore they hated to see Nehemiah arriving to assist the Jews in the work.

Upon reaching Jerusalem, Nehemiah (like Ezra before him) rested for three days, doubtless spending a considerable

---

[7] C. F. Keil and Franz Delitzsch, *Biblical Commentary on the Old Testament*, VIII, 168.

portion of the time in prayer. Then he made a most important night survey (vv. 12-16). Up to this point he had not
revealed his true purpose for coming to anyone in the land.
Before he did, he made a careful inspection of the wall in
a manner calculated to attract as little publicity as possible
—by night, just a few companions with him, no animal
except the one he himself was riding.

Nehemiah left Jerusalem by the valley gate on the west
side of the city. No one now knows the exact location of the
dragon ("jackal," ASV) well. He then rode on to the dung
port at the southwest corner of the city where refuse from
the city streets was taken out. The walls on this side of
Jerusalem he found to be "broken down," the gates themselves "consumed with fire." He then traveled to the southeast corner of the city where "the gate of the fountain" was
located. Just inside this was the reservoir, called "the king's
pool." At this point, because of the rubbish, the beast he
was riding had to be abandoned.

Nehemiah next traversed the east side of the city, walk-
ing along the brook Kidron. During most of the year the
bed of this brook was completely dry, but in the rainy season it became a torrent. Beyond it lay the Mount of Olives.
From the side of the stream he could get a complete view
of the condition of the walls along the east. Then Nehemiah
apparently retraced his steps, going back in by the same gate
from which he had left the city. It is specifically stated that
he had not up to this time told any of the leaders, people
or workmen of his idea for rebuilding the walls. His night
survey convinced him of the complete feasibility of his
plan.

Now this man of God was ready to exhort the people to

reconstruct the walls (vv. 17-18). He called the rulers, and
to them he spoke of their distress due to the wasted condition of city and walls. Reminding them that because of this
they were an object of reproach to their enemies, he urged
them to get busy and build the wall. But notice that he did
not say, "*You* are a reproach; *you* are in distress; *you* build."
He said instead, "*We* . . . let *us* build." Then he informed
them of God's previous blessing in giving him the favor of
the king and the benefit of his authority. This exhortation
brought such encouragement to their hearts that they agreed
with Nehemiah, saying, "Let us rise up and build" (v. 18).
And they were as good as their word; they immediately
began in an energetic way to get busy on the job.

As soon as they did, opposition arose. Enemies made an
attack, first by ridicule, then by false accusation. Involved
with Sanballat and Tobiah in this opposition was another
enemy now introduced for the first time, Geshem the Arab-
ian (v. 19).

> Sanballat, Tobiah, and Geshem are united so closely,
> and act so much together . . . that it is difficult to sup-
> pose them to be three chieftains residing on three sides of
> Judaea . . . merely holding diplomatic intercourse with
> each other, which is the ordinary idea.[8]

Possibly, Geshem was "the head of a body of Arab troops
maintained by Sanballat at Samaria."[9]

First these opponents ridiculed the attempts of the Jews
to rebuild their wall. Afterward they accused them of false
motives, of plotting rebellion against the king and rebuilding
the fortifications of the city for this purpose. The same

---

[8] *Pulpit Commentary*, VII, 19.
[9] *Ibid.*

charge had been directed against the Jews in Zerubbabel's time (see Ezra 4).

Nehemiah's answer was brief but dignified. He identified the Israelites as servants of "the God of heaven," calmly asserting that they were going to rebuild. He made it clear that the opposition on the part of the Samaritans was simply a matter of "sour grapes." They had been refused any right or portion in Jerusalem, so now through jealousy they wanted to wreck the work.

BUILDING THE WALL (3:1-32)

This chapter contains yet another of those great honor rolls of faith which are to be found interspersed in the Bible. Also, it has been said that this one chapter contains a greater amount of information concerning the topography of ancient Jerusalem than do all other passages put together. Ten gates of the city are here mentioned, and the story of building the wall centers around them.

The first of these is "the sheep gate" (vv. 1-2), which was located on Jerusalem's northeast side, just north of the temple area. It is thought that it was called this because by it the sheep for sacrifices were brought in.

At the time the work on the walls began, Eliashib, the grandson of Joshua, was high priest. He led the other priests in rebuilding the sheep gate. Near the gate were two towers, Meah and Hananeel. Next to the priests the men of Jericho helped build, and beyond them Zaccur, the son of Imri, worked.

When individuals are, like Zaccur, mentioned in the following description . . . as builders or repairers of portions

of wall, they are heads of houses who engaged in the work
of building at the head of the fathers of families and individuals who were dependent on them.[10]

The fish gate (vv. 3-5) is mentioned in several other portions of Scripture. Apparently the fish market was located
nearby and fish were brought in through this gate from the
Mediterranean. Among those helping in the construction in
this area of the wall were the Tekoites, people of Tekoa.
Their nobles, however, refused to assist in the work, so obviously not all supported Nehemiah in his project, though
the majority did. Even today we have spiritual descendants
of these Tekoites in our churches! While they are willing to
enjoy the benefits of the work of the church, they refuse to
take any active part themselves.

Next was the old gate (vv. 6-12). The reason is uncertain
for calling it thus. Verse 7 speaks of the building extending
"unto the throne of the governor on this side the river."
Evidently the governor of the entire area west of the Euphrates had in this locality a judgment seat which he used
while in Jerusalem, much as did Pilate at a considerably
later time.

Rephaiah (v. 9) is termed "the ruler of the half part of
Jerusalem," which is better rendered "half the district of
Jerusalem" (ASV). The reference is to the area outside the
city, but still under Jerusalem control. Jedaiah (v. 10) repaired the part "over against his house," wisely starting
with the work which was near at hand. Sometimes, sad to
say, people have a desire to work for God in far distant
places but seem unwilling to serve right at home.

---

[10] Keil and Delitzsch, p. 176.

The "tower of the furnaces" (v. 11) was possibly the place where the bakers had their ovens. Verse 12 speaks of "Shallum . . . and his daughters." Can it be that women also took an active part in the construction? Some say no and explain the term as figurative of towns in the man's district. Others speculate that his daughters were women of wealth and hired men to do the actual work at this particular spot.

The valley gate (v. 13) and the wall for a distance of fifteen hundred feet to the dung gate (v. 14) were repaired by the people of Zanoah, a small town ten miles to the west.

The fountain gate came next (vv. 15-25). The king's pool, or reservoir, at this gate connected with the pool of Siloah (or Siloam). Beyond this were stairs which led to the palace of David, which was situated just behind the water gate (v. 26). Special honorable mention is given to Baruch (v. 20) who was so careful and diligent with his work that it is said he "earnestly repaired."

Verse 26 evidently means that the Nethinim helped in the repair of the area around the water gate. This section of Jerusalem was called Ophel (v. 27). Beyond this was the horse gate (v. 28), a gate at the southeast corner of the temple through which horses could enter. Priests lived in this area and repaired this portion of the wall.

The east gate (v. 29) was the main entrance into the temple from the Mount of Olives. It was also called the Shushan gate and the beautiful gate (Acts 3:2).[11]

The exact location of the gate Miphkad (vv. 31-32) is un-

---

[11] "The main entrance from the Mount of Olives and the Kidron Valley into the Temple was by this gate built into Solomon's porch. It was called Shushan because it was adorned with a representation of the Palace of Shushan, probably in commemoration of Daniel's vision, when he was comforted by an angel concerning the restoration of the Jews (Dan. 8:2). It was at Shushan also that Zerubbabel was commissioned to rebuild the Temple, and Nehemiah Jerusalem (Neh. 1:1). In the Palace there, Esther was chosen queen and Mordecai promoted. The carving was so exquisite, that the Gate was also called Beautiful (Acts 3:2, 10)" (D. A. Thompson, *Jerusalem and the Temples in Bible History and Prophecy*, p. 27).

known, but it must have been somewhere around the north-east section of the wall. The name is said to mean "gate of judgment."

H. A. Ironside makes an unusual but helpful spiritual application of these gates, in the order in which they come.[12] It is not claimed that there is typical or symbolical teaching intended here, but simply that a practical spiritual application can be derived. The first gate mentioned in the chapter is the sheep gate. This naturally suggests the cross to one familiar with the Bible, and the sacrifice upon it of the Lamb of God. This gate was built by a priest; Christ offered Himself for us as our great High Priest (Heb. 7:26-27). Then came the fish gate, which brings to mind the Lord's pro-mise "I will make you fishers of men" (Matt. 4:19). The one saved through Christ's blood is himself to become an evangelist, winning others to the Lord. The old gate sug-gests subjection to the revealed will of God (Jer. 6:16). The valley gate makes us think of humility (Ps. 84:6); the dung gate of cleansing from defilement (I John 1:7-9). The fountain gate brings to our thoughts sanctification by the Spirit and by the Word of God (Eph. 5:25-26). The water gate, which seems to have been still intact, reminds one of the Word of God which needs no repair. The horse gate speaks of war (the horse being used then as an animal of warfare), which brings to mind the judgments of the tribu-lation period (Rev. 6:1-8), and also of One who will return from heaven on "a white horse" (Rev. 19:11). The east gate points to the coming day when the "Sun of righteousness" rises (Mal. 4:2). The Miphkad gate, the "gate of judgment," should make us meditate on "the judgment seat of Christ"

[12] See H. A. Ironside, *Notes on Ezra, Nehemiah and Esther*, pp. 24-52.

before which all believers must some day stand (II Cor. 5:10).

In Nehemiah 12:39 two other gates are mentioned: the gate of Ephraim and the prison gate. Apparently these gates did not need repairing and thus are not mentioned in the third chapter. The ten in chapter 3, plus the two in chapter 12, total twelve gates in all. In the New Jerusalem (Rev. 21:12) there are also twelve gates.

Observe that the incidents related in chapters 4 and 5 took place at the same time as the building described in chapter 3. These chapters, now to be considered, reveal that while construction was going forward on the wall, constant opposition was being endured by the builders.

THE WORK CONTINUES DESPITE OPPOSITION (4:1-23)

Opposition by Ridicule (vv. 1-6)

When he learned that construction on the wall was progressing in a systematic, businesslike way, Sanballat became exceedingly angry and indignant. His first recourse was to mockery. Before his friends and the Samaritan army (a sort of local militia) he openly scorned the Jews as feeble weaklings. His tirade was in the form of a series of sarcastic questions, all implying that they would never be able to fortify the city. Sanballat suggested that the foolish Jews apparently thought that all they would have to do was make a sacrifice to Jehovah and He would enable them to finish their project in a day. He intimated that they stupidly thought they could use the rubbish and burned-out stones of the old wall to build a substantial new structure.

Tobiah took up the jest and carried it further. As there were doubtless many foxes (or jackals) living in the ruined sections of Jerusalem, he laughingly asserted that even if such a small creature as that should run against the wall (when it was completed) it would fall down because of its flimsy construction. Someone has commented that it later proved adequate to withstand such "foxes" as these men were!

When Nehemiah heard of this, his response was to turn to God (vv. 4-5). He certainly must have been a real man of prayer, as this is one of eight brief prayers recorded in his short book.[13] The only "long" prayer is that of 1:5-11. This particular prayer is very much like the so-called "imprecatory psalms."[14] These psalms are called this because they contain prayers for the overthrow and defeat of the wicked. Critics have argued that such petitions have no place in a really holy book. Recall, however, that they were uttered during a different age from ours, that of law, and were in perfect harmony with the law which said, "An eye for an eye, and a tooth for a tooth." Nehemiah simply prayed that what these adversaries had tried to do to the Israelites might come instead on themselves. He also prayed that the Lord would definitely deal with them because of their sin. He really was indignant because these evil men had spoken against God Himself. And this had been done not privately but publicly, so that all the builders heard of it.

Despite ridicule and threat, the labor continued unabated until eventually the wall was half completed, that is, was completed halfway up to the intended height. Observe that

---

[13] For the others, see 2:4; 5:19; 6:9, 14; 13:14, 22, 29.
[14] See G. Coleman Luck, *The Bible Book by Book*, pp. 86-87.

the reason such rapid progress was made was because "the people had a mind to work." Such a spirit is sorely needed among God's people today, as there is much work to be done.

The *Pulpit Commentary* states that a mind to work springs from such things as a sense of duty, a sense of necessity concerning tasks which must be accomplished, from gratitude and love to God the Father and Christ our Redeemer, from benevolence toward others, from hope of accomplishing good and obtaining good, and from the encouragement of faithful leaders such as Nehemiah. A mind to work displays itself in the very laboring which will be prompt, hearty, happy, abundant, steady and persevering despite difficulties. A mind to work produces freedom from unhealthy thoughts and actions, growth in true Christian life, and success.

> No instruments, however cunningly devised and well-made, will do much without the "mind to work"; but with our mind in the work we can do almost anything with such weapons as we have at hand.[15]

Opposition by Threat of Open Attack (4:7-9)

When they saw that the work was advancing exceedingly well, Sanballat and Tobiah turned from ridicule to open attack. First they made alliances with other enemies of the Jews—Arabians, Ammonites, Philistines from Ashdod—planning to attack with an army and bring the project forcibly to a halt.

Receiving information about this threat, Nehemiah and his companions first of all prayed. But they also began to exert greater care. They set a watch day and night, with the evident intention of defending themselves should these adversaries make a warlike attempt to stop the construction. If they had simply prayed and then had proceeded in a careless way, that would have been presumption rather than faith. If a student today should pray that God would enable him to do well in his schoolwork and then be careless and negligent in his own study and preparation, would that be an example of real faith?

Opposition from Discouragement (v. 10)

After this the Jews themselves became generally discouraged. Complaints became common, their strength was weakened (possibly by using some as watchmen rather than laborers) and there was so much rubbish that they couldn't build the wall. The halfway point is usually the most crucial time in any work of an extended nature. By that time the original enthusiasm has waned and the final burst of zeal which is produced by the thought that the job is almost completed has not yet arisen. As to the complaint of the Jews, the rubbish certainly was not greater in quantity then when they started and built the first half of the wall. Indeed, it surely must have been less!

Opposition from the Threat of Secret Attack (vv. 11-23)

The Samaritans and their allies now began to spread the report that very shortly they would fall on the Jews in secret attack, so that before the Jews realized what was happening they would be in their midst slaughtering the workers and forcing the endeavor to cease. Such reports were brought to Nehemiah a number of times by the Jews residing closest to the Samaritans. The statement of these border dwellers (v. 12b) is not perfectly clear in its meaning. Did they mean that the contingents of workers from their locality ought to stop work on the wall and return to protect their homes? Or did they intend to express the thought that the enemies would fall on the builders in many places disrupting the work?

Whatever the case, Nehemiah's reaction to this was to place groups of men with weapons at the lower points of the wall as far as it had been constructed. These guards were set on high spots where they could easily be seen over the low wall by the enemies. Nehemiah's statement in verse 14 sounds very much as though he looked on one occasion and saw the adversaries actually advancing in the distance. He then arose and exhorted the rulers and the rest of the people not to be afraid, urging them to remember the Lord and to fight valiantly for Him and for their families. The result was that the attackers, when they saw that the Israelites were well prepared for them, called off their charge and left the Jews to return to their task of building.

From that time forward, Nehemiah had half of his own personal servants and bodyguard assist with the work. The other half he had ready with weapons to rush to any point where attack threatened. The rulers remained behind the workers, both directing and encouraging them. Those with the job of loading and carrying materials handled them with one hand and kept a sword in the other. Those who by necessity had to use both hands in building, nevertheless still kept their swords in close reach by their sides.

A trumpeter stood by Nehemiah ready to sound the alarm should danger threaten. It was arranged that where-ever the builders heard the sound of the trumpet, they would all rush to that spot to face the enemy. Thus the work went forward. The laborers began at the rising of the sun and worked each day until the stars appeared. Nehemiah called on the out-of-town workers to remain in the city instead of going back each night to their homes so that they could help guard the walls. During this crucial period he himself never removed his clothes except for the purpose of washing them. The same thing was true of his brothers, servants and guardsmen.

The Work Hindered by Selfishness and Greed (5:1-19)

The next obstacle to the work came from the inside rather than the outside. The poorer people raised a cry against their wealthier brethren. Their work on the wall brought them no pay and this, added to other conditions, caused them to be financially hard pressed. Their families were large (v. 2) and food of course had to be provided for them. There had been a severe drought (v. 3), which had forced them to mortgage their lands to obtain provisions. Also they had to pay a considerable tax to the king of Persia (v. 4). Though they loved their children equally as much as the wealthy money lenders did theirs, yet they were being forced to sell them into bondage to meet their debts. Others were getting possession of both their lands and children, which they lacked the power to redeem.

Nehemiah was greatly angered when this complaint reached him. He was especially indignant that at such a crucial time, when all needed to closely cooperate, the wealthy nobles should be pressing and dispossessing their poverty-stricken countrymen. After thinking the matter over, he had a conference with these nobles, rebuking them for exacting usury from the poorer people (v. 7). This was indeed a sin against the Mosaic law (see Lev. 25:35-37). Such a sin is often committed even today against the poor and ignorant.

Evidently the private rebuke of the nobles produced little result, so Nehemiah then proceeded to call a public assembly where he again upbraided them. He indicated that he and his brethren had been redeeming Jews sold in bondage to their heathen neighbors, so far as financial ability permitted. Then he pointedly asked the nobles if they were now going to do just the opposite—sell their brethren into bondage, not to the heathen but to other Jews. Too ashamed to make reply, the nobles held their peace. So Nehemiah further showed them that their conduct was not good; in fact it was especially bad in view of the difficult situation which faced the whole nation. He and his brothers had loaned money too and could if they wished have exacted exorbitant interest from the people. But this they had not done.

He called on the nobles to cease their usury and to restore any homes they had taken from the poor people. They also were told to restore the interest they had collected which was said to have been "the hundreth part of the money" (v. 11). Evidently they were charging 1 percent per month on these loans, or 12 percent interest per year.

This exhortation touched the nobles and they promised to do that which Nehemiah asked. He then called the priests and had them witness the oath of the nobles that they would carry out his instructions. He also pronounced a curse on anyone who broke this oath. Gathering his robes into a kind of bag, Nehemiah then shook them out on the floor, calling on God to thus shake out from his home and possessions each one who did not keep the oath. At the close of the meeting the whole company praised God that the matter had been thus settled. It is recorded that the promises made were actually kept.

Verses 14-19 give a summary of Nehemiah's conduct during his entire term as governor, which makes it evident that the account in these opening chapters of the book was written by Nehemiah after he had completed the twelve years in office. The incident of his dealing with the greedy money lenders led him at this point to summarize his own actions, so opposite in nature, during his entire administration. He makes it clear that during the dozen years neither he nor his brothers took any pay whatever from the people. Former governors had their expenses cared for by taxes of both money and wine from the general public. While the Bible records the names of only two previous governors, Zerubbabel and Ezra, it is evident that in the hundred years since the first return there had been a number of others.

In this matter, Nehemiah did not think he had to follow the usual custom: "But so did not I, because of the fear of God" (v. 15). Today people often attempt to excuse questionable actions by the claim that "everybody does it." Thank God, Nehemiah did not live by such a principle! The fact that other governors took certain things as their due did not at all influence him. The main motive power in his life was not custom but "the fear of God." This is said in Scripture to be "the beginning of wisdom" (Ps. 111:10; Prov. 9:10). He refrained from doing some things because a reverential fear of the Lord made him anxious not to displease Him. This same feeling should be a strong motivating force in our own lives. "Knowing therefore the terror [fear] of the Lord, we persuade men" (II Cor. 5:11).

Nehemiah had all his servants help in the wall building. He and his relatives did not buy up the land from poor people who were in financial straits in order to make high profits. As a matter of fact, he was very generous in entertaining people at his own table, both Jerusalem residents and visiting Jews from other lands. In this connection he recounted the amount of food he used for such a purpose. But despite all this he still did not take anything from the people for himself, knowing that their taxes to Persia were heavy. Nehemiah was evidently a man of independent wealth at the time he first came to Jerusalem.

All of these things he did, not because he sought the praise of men, but rather, because he desired to receive the rewards of the God he always endeavored to please. "Think upon me, my God, for good" (v. 19).

THE WALL COMPLETED (6:1-19)

For a little time while the Jews were quarreling among themselves, it appears that Sanballat and his gang held their peace. But soon they learned that the construction was again going on apace. The breaks in the wall had finally all been closed and the time for the gates to be fastened in was drawing near.

Once more the enemies attempted to hinder the work by deceit. They invited Nehemiah to meet with them at a point some distance away so they could settle their differences at a friendly conference. But the man of God recognized right away that this was a mere trick, for their real intention was to lure him away from his friends so that they could harm and possibly even kill him. He refused to heed the hypocritical request. Why should he stop to talk with them when he was "doing a great work"? Four times they sent for him to come, and on each occasion he rejected their invitation.

When this scheme failed, Sanballat proceeded to pen an "open letter" (vv. 5-9). When he sent the fifth time for Nehemiah, his servant brought this "open letter," a communication in some way made open to the public, so that not only Nehemiah but everyone in the city of Jerusalem could read it. Such letters are even now on certain occasions printed in newspapers. It is obvious that as a general rule they are written for the express purpose of making trouble. Sanballat's was worded in a most subtle manner as if he were a true friend of Nehemiah desirous only of helping him. He stated that there was a report among the Gentiles that Nehemiah and the Jews were planning to rebel against the Persian king and make Nehemiah himself their ruler. In fact, it was said, according to Sanballat, that prophets had already been engaged by Nehemiah to proclaim that he was the king of Judah. Sanballat stated that he felt it his duty to inform the king of Persia about this, but wished first to confer with Nehemiah to hear his side of the matter.

Nehemiah immediately answered Sanballat, writing him bluntly that the whole story was a fabrication concocted by Sanballat himself.

Thus in various ways these enemies tried to terrorize the faithful Jews into discontinuing their work. Nehemiah closes the paragraph with one of his brief but fervent prayers: "Now therefore, O God, strengthen my hands" (v. 9b).

Before the wall was finished, one final attempt was made by the adversaries to thwart the work (vv. 10-14). One of the Jews, claiming to be a prophet, advised Nehemiah that he had received a prophecy which indicated an attempt would be made that night on Nehemiah's life. It is not perfectly clear as to why Nehemiah went to Shemaiah's house, nor is it known for certain the meaning of "shut up" (v. 10). One view holds that the reference is to Shemaiah as being ceremonially unclean and not able at the moment to leave his home. Another is that he had shut himself up in pretended fear of the supposed assassins. Whatever the case, it is plainly stated that he called on Nehemiah to go with him and hide in the temple, apparently meaning in the holy place itself, in order to be safe.

Verse 11 in the Authorized Version indicates that Nehemiah scorned to hide in cowardly fear, knowing himself to be a leader with God's hand upon him. The American Standard Version margin reads: "Who is there, that, being such as I, could go into the temple and live?" Possibly this is nearer to the original thought—that Nehemiah, not being a priest, could not lawfully enter the holy place of the temple.

Later Nehemiah discerned that Shemaiah was not a true prophet at all, but had actually been hired by Tobiah to attempt to intimidate Nehemiah into committing the sin of unlawfully entering the holy place. Then a most damaging charge could have been circulated against Nehemiah that he had committed a serious sin through cowardice.

Nehemiah's influence depended greatly on the weight of his moral character. One false step and he would have been lost; his influence would have been gone; and the work on which his heart was set would have come to naught.[16]

Again a brief prayer uttered by Nehemiah is recorded (v. 14). He prayed that God would reward these evil deceivers "according to these their works." Other prophets are mentioned (and also a prophetess, Noadiah), who evidently were also bribed to terrorize Nehemiah.

The completion of the wall is recorded in verses 15-16. Despite all the cunning opposition, the work was finally finished in slightly less than two months. Critics of the Bible have asserted that this period of time is too brief to be credible. However, it must not be overlooked that the people themselves had "a mind to work," while over and above this God was with them, supernaturally blessing the labor. Other factors of importance also should be considered. There was a large force of workmen, not only from Jerusalem but from all the outlying villages. The ruins of the previous wall contained large quantities of stones, and it is quite possible that additional materials had also been stockpiled before the work actually began.

When the various Gentile opponents around Judah learned of the success of Nehemiah, they were "much cast down in their own eyes." They no longer felt so important as they once did, and were quite humiliated. At last they were forced to recognize and admit that the blessing of God was truly on the work of the Jews. Oh, that modern-day opponents of the gospel might have a similar experience!

The closing verses of the chapter (and section) apparently refer to the period of construction rather than to the time after the wall was finished. It is explained that Tobiah had

[16] *Ibid.*, p. 63.

many friends in Jerusalem, as he had married a Jewish woman and his son Johanan had done likewise. Tobiah's Israel-
itish allies continually received letters from him and then
did their best to impress Nehemiah with Tobiah's sincerity,
probably urging an alliance between the two. These people
also reported the plans of Nehemiah to Tobiah.

2

SPIRITUAL REVIVAL (7:1–10:39)

The wall having been completed, and assignments of Levites to their posts having been made, Nehemiah evidently contemplated returning to Persia. So provision was made for rule during his absence. He appointed Hanani his brother, and Hananiah the officer in charge of the fortress adjoining the temple, to be corulers while he was away. It is specified that Hananiah was given this important post because he was such a faithful, godly man.

Instructions were also given regarding the gates. They were not to be opened at sunrise, which was the usual custom in that day, but only after the sun was well up. Then at the close of the day the gates were to be shut and barred. In addition, the people of Jerusalem were not to become careless now that the wall was completed, but were to keep watch for enemies from their own houses. Nehemiah doubtless remembered that Babylon, despite its mighty walls, had fallen to the Persians due to lack of watchfulness.

Now that his main task was completed, Nehemiah also noticed that the population of Jerusalem was quite small in comparison with the size of the territory enclosed in the walls. In much of the area, the houses had never been rebuilt.

NEHEMIAH PREPARES TO TAKE A CENSUS, AND FINDS THE
REGISTER OF THOSE WHO RETURNED
WITH ZERUBBABEL (7:5-73)

As a first step toward remedying the uninhabited condition of the city, Nehemiah undertook to make a census of
all the people. In his preparations for this he found a copy
of the register of the original group of returnees. This copy
he placed in his own record at this point. Except for certain
slight differences, it is a duplication of the list in Ezra 2 (see
comment on these differences in the author's discussion of
that chapter). It has been suggested that the list in Ezra's
book was prepared in Babylon of those who expected to return, while the one given by Nehemiah was made in Jerusalem itself of those who actually *did* return. This could account for the small variations.

EZRA TEACHES THE LAW (8:1-12)

This chapter opens by telling how Ezra read the law to
the people (vv. 1-3). Ezra's name was not in the first six
chapters of Nehemiah's book and was last referred to in the
final chapter of his own writing. If he had been present
during the time of the wall building, it would indeed be
strange if he had not in some way assisted in that great project. It would also be hard to imagine that he could have
been present in Jerusalem all the time since the close of his
own book and yet have allowed spiritual conditions to reach
such a low ebb as Nehemiah discovered when he first returned. Surely the theory must be correct which supposes
that Ezra was recalled to Persia shortly after the events with
which his book concluded, and returned to Jerusalem for
the first time after the wall had been completed. Would it

not then be natural that the people, divinely impelled to gather in the city, would once again ask their former leader Ezra to read the Scriptures to them?

The reading was done on the first day of the seventh month. In a large open square before the water gate, Ezra read the law of Moses, the Torah (or Pentateuch) from early morning until noon. This reading must then have lasted some five or six hours. It was done before a great crowd of men, women, and even children who were old enough to understand. Unlike some Christians when the Word of God is read in services today, the people had "attentive ears," which means that they listened very closely to the Word.

A special pulpit large enough to hold not only Ezra but thirteen others was constructed of wood (v. 4). These thirteen apparently assisted him in the long period of reading. When he opened the book, the people, showing their respect for the Word of God, stood up. Then Ezra blessed the Lord, the people answering "amen" and bowing in worship. Another thirteen men are mentioned in verse 7 who also assisted Ezra and "caused the people to understand the law." "They read . . . and gave the sense" (v. 8). Some understand this to mean that the Jews then present could not perfectly understand the more ancient Hebrew in which the Pentateuch was written and had to have the message translated into Aramaic, the dialect which they had become accustomed to speak while in Babylon. Militating against this view is the fact that Haggai, Zechariah and Malachi are all in Hebrew, as well as the larger portion of Daniel and Ezra. Surely all these books were not written in a language incomprehensible except to a scholarly minority!

The view seems more acceptable which holds that "giving the sense" and "causing the people to understand" are references to popular exposition being given from time to time of the portions of Scripture which had been read. "It would seem almost as if there were first a public reading, and then a separation of the assembly into groups, while the appointed Levites explained and enforced the terms of the Law."[1]

When the people heard the law they wept, realizing how they had broken it (vv. 9-12). However, Nehemiah and Ezra urged them not to mourn. The day was that of the Feast of Trumpets, an occasion of rejoicing, not of sadness.[2] Ezra told them to go and feast instead, especially remembering the poor. When the Levites also encouraged them in the same direction, the people did as they were advised.

THE FEAST OF TABERNACLES IS OBSERVED (8:13-18)

It is an almost invariable rule that earnest listening to the clear teaching of God's Word whets the spiritual appetite for more. Thus it was with these Israelites of the restoration period. On the second day they came back to hear Ezra read again. By this time the reading had advanced to Leviticus 23. There they learned that the Feast of Tabernacles was to be observed by their dwelling in booths. This feast began on the fifteenth day of the seventh month, and was one of the three appointed seasons which all Israel was commanded to celebrate (see Exodus 23:14-17; Deut. 16:16).

---

[1] G. Campbell Morgan, *An Exposition of the Whole Bible*, p. 194.
[2] "The Feast of Trumpets was distinguished for its joy and gladness. . . . The feast of the memorial of the Trumpets was intended to rouse the nation of joyful anticipation and to summon their attention. It was to awaken and quicken the national expectations, and to prepare the people for the great day [of Atonement] so near at hand. It was an appeal to men to avail themselves of the provision made for their reconciliation with God—an appeal to be reconciled with him" (W. G. Moorehead, *Studies in Mosaic Institutions*, pp. 225-26).

It was decided that they would keep the feast exactly as the law had prescribed, so booths were constructed of tree branches. The city dwellers made their booths on the flat tops of their houses. The country people placed theirs in the courts and in the streets. The result was that not since the days of Joshua had there been such glorious celebrating of the Feast of Tabernacles. On each of the seven days of the period, the people continued with the Bible reading and exposition by Ezra. On the eighth day of the feast "a solemn assembly" was held. This day would have been the twenty-second of the seventh month. The scene with which chapter 9 opens must then have occurred just two days after that with which chapter 8 closes.

REVIVAL COMES (9:1-38)

Because of the nature of the season, the people had previously been restrained from the sorrow they felt on learning how far they had strayed from God's holy law. Now that the Feast of Tabernacles was over, they met once again— this time for fasting and confession of sin (vv.1-3). In connection with their grief, "sackclothes" and "earth" are mentioned. Sackcloth, a coarse rough material made of goat's hair, was often worn in that day to indicate mourning.[3] Less frequently dust was thrown on the head for the same purpose.[4] Separating themselves from those who were not God's people, the Israelites confessed that they had sinned and had followed the iniquitous way of their ancestors. Once more there was a time of Bible reading, lasting for three hours. Then there was a period of similar length devoted to confession of sin.

[3] See Gen. 37:34; II Sam. 3:31; 21:10; I Kings 21:27.
[4] See I Sam. 4:12; II Sam. 1:2; Job 2:12.

At the close of this general time of confession a number of Levites "stood up upon the stairs" (raised platforms at various places in the assembly) and "with a loud voice" led the people in a most beautiful prayer (vv. 4-38). If all these Levites repeated this same prayer, then obviously it must have been written ahead of time. Very likely it was composed by Ezra himself as it sounds quite similar to his great prayer in Ezra 9.

This prayer of the Levites is the longest one recorded in the entire Bible. Beginning with praise of God as the mighty Creator (vv. 5-6), it recounts much of the history of Israel. Features included are the call of Abraham (vv. 7-8); the deliverance from Egypt (vv. 9-11); the leading through the wilderness by pillar of cloud and fire (v. 12); the giving of the law at Mount Sinai (vv. 13-14). Then the prayer goes on to speak of the provision of God during the wilderness journey (v. 15); the rebellion against Jehovah and worship of the golden calf (vv. 16-18); the mercy of the Lord even after that, as displayed in the forty years of wandering (vv. 19-21). Finally reference is made to the conquest of the land during the time of Joshua (vv. 22-25); then their disobedience and failure in the period of the judges and later of the prophets (vv. 26-30).

After this recounting of Israel's history, there comes a striking confession of sin followed by an appeal to the Lord for succor in distress (vv. 31-38). The long prayer closes with the promise of "a sure covenant" that the people desire to make with God. It is said that the princes, Levites and priests would sign this covenant for the people.

A Covenant Is Made To Be Faithful to God (10:1-39)

The final verse of chapter nine makes reference to a covenant: "Because of all this we make a sure covenant, and write it; and our princes, Levites, and priests, seal unto it." In 10:1-27 the signers of this solemn agreement are listed. First comes the name of the Tirshatha (governor). The word Tirshatha is from a Persian root meaning "his severity," and evidently was then used for high officials, somewhat as "his excellency" is used. After the Tirshatha come the names of the various heads of houses.

Verses 28-29 sum up the balance of the people—all who had separated themselves unto God—all who were old enough to understand—men, women and children. These "clave to their brethren, their nobles" who had signed the covenant. All solemnly promised to keep the agreement, to "walk in God's law."

The seven provisions of the covenant are itemized in verses 30-39. These stipulated that (1) none would marry heathen (v. 30); (2) that all would observe the Sabbath (v. 31a); and (3) observe the Sabbatic year (v. 31b); (4) pay the temple tax (vv. 32-33); (5) supply wood for the temple altar (v. 34); (6) give the priests and Levites their due (vv. 35-38); not forsake God's house (v. 39).

3

FURTHER REFORMS (11:1–13:31)

Earlier in the book the statement was made that the population of Jerusalem, the capital city, was too small: "Now the city was large and great: but the people were few therein, and the houses were not builded" (7:4). Nehemiah evidently numbered all the people and then decided that 10 percent of those living in the remainder of the country should dwell in Jerusalem. Of this number some were chosen by lot; others volunteered to come willingly, and these received the praise of all the rest of the people.

Verses 3-19 contain a list of some of the chief families dwelling in Jerusalem at the time, while verses 20-24 mention other inhabitants of the city: Nethinims, Levites, etc. The chapter closes with a record of the towns and villages outside Jerusalem (vv. 25-35).

The first group consists of the heads of families of priests and Levites who came up to Jerusalem with Zerubbabel in the original return (vv. 1-9).

Why this register should be here inserted by Nehemiah does not appear, perhaps to keep in remembrance those good men, that posterity might know to whom they were

beholden, under God, for the happy revival and reestablishment of their religion among them. Thus must we contri-
bute toward the performance of that promise, Ps. cxii. 6,
The righteous shall be in everlasting remembrance. . . .
Perhaps it is intended to stir up their posterity, who succeeded them in the priest's office and inherited their digni-
ties and preferments, to imitate their courage and fidelity.[1]

Of special interest is the list of high priests from Joshua
to Jaddua (vv. 10-11). According to Josephus, the high
priest who received Alexander the Great into Jerusalem was
named Jaddua.[2] Although the time of this event was about
a century after the close of Nehemiah's book, it is not impossible that it could be the same Jaddua here mentioned.
He may have been a tiny baby at the moment Nehemiah
wrote these words, but nevertheless in the direct line of the
high priesthood and therefore included.

The heads of the priestly courses during the high priesthood of Joiakim are next itemized (vv. 12-21). Finally, a
record is included of the chief Levites who served during
the period specified in verse 26: "These were in the days of
Joiakim the son of Jeshua, the son of Jozadak, and in the
days of Nehemiah the governor, and of Ezra the priest,
the scribe."

THE DEDICATION OF THE WALL (12:27-47)

An impressive service was eventually held to celebrate
the completion of the walls. This is described in verses 27-
43. For this occasion many instrumentalists and singers
were assembled for a notable ministry of music. The priests
purified themselves, the wall, the gates and the people.

[1] Matthew Henry, *Commentary on the Whole Bible*, II, 1111.
[2] Josephus, *Antiquities of the Jews*. XI. 7. 4-5.

This was probably done, judging from the analogy of 2 Chron. xxix. 20, by the offering of sin-offerings and burnt-offerings, according to some special ritual unknown to us, as sacrifices of purification and dedication.[3]

Remember that during the dispensation of law, even lifeless things such as buildings could become ceremonially defiled (see e.g., Deut. 23:14; Lev. 14:34-53; 16:16).

Next Nehemiah divided the people into "two great companies" (v. 31). All apparently met about midway on the western wall. Then one company led by Ezra marched around the south wall and on up the east wall. The other group, under Nehemiah's leadership, paraded around the north wall and on down the east wall. At some midway point on this eastern wall the two companies met and marched into the house of God, all the while singing and giving thanks to the Lord. Many sacrifices were then offered in the temple. In the city there was such great rejoicing among men, women and children that the sound of "the joy of Jerusalem was heard even afar off" (v. 43).

Chapter 12 closes with a comment on the way in which tithes were collected for the priests and Levites at this period, and how these men performed their respective duties (vv. 44-47).

NEHEMIAH'S RETURN TO JERUSALEM AND HIS CORRECTION OF DISORDERS THERE (13:1-31)

As already indicated, even before the dedicatory service, Nehemiah was planning his return to Shushan. Obviously after the joyful event was over, he did go back to Persia and was gone for a length of time impossible now to determine

[3] C. F. Keil and Franz Delitzsch, *Biblical Commentary on the Old Testament,* VIII, 275.

(see 13:6). "On that day" (13:1) may first seem to refer to the day of dedication pictured in chapter 12, but 13:10 shows that such a conjecture is erroneous. On the "day" of chapter 13, the Levites were not given their portion, whereas this had been done at the time of dedication (12:47). So chapter 13 records events which took place a considerable time after the close of chapter 12.

"On that day" then refers to the day of Nehemiah's return to Jerusalem after a lengthy absence. Once more the people met, as of old, for a reading of "the book of Moses." The particular statement which they found there is actually from Deuteronomy 23:3-4, further proof that the first five books of the Old Testament (the Pentateuch) were considered as a unit by the Jews, and the whole was spoken of as "the book of Moses." This is also excellent evidence for the Mosaic authorship of the Pentateuch.

The text that especially caused heart-searching among the people was one which sharply separated the Israelites from the Moabites and Ammonites. Sad to say, a number had once more intermarried with the heathen of the area, and a separation such as that described in the last chapter of Ezra had to be made once more.

One of the chief offenders in such matters was the high priest Eliashib himself (vv. 4-9). He had allied himself to Tobiah the Ammonite, a chief hinderer to the building of the wall, and secretary to the governor of Samaria. And he had even brazenly provided a large room in the courts of the temple for Tobiah, who had put a lot of "household stuff" there. When he learned this, Nehemiah's dismay was great; he says, "It grieved me sore" (v. 8). This stern man of action proceeded to pitch all of Tobiah's equipment out of

the chamber. Then he had the whole suite of rooms purified
from the desecration and restored to its former use, a store-
place for materials and vessels used in the sacrifices.

Nehemiah's investigation next revealed that the tithes had
not been regularly collected (v. 10). As a result the Levites,
temple workers and musicians had not been paid. This
forced them to leave their service in the house of God and
spend all their time tilling their section of land in an attempt
to make a living for themselves and their families.

Nehemiah "contended" about this matter with the rulers,
whose responsibility it was to see to the collection of the
tithes. After sufficiently straightening them out, he sought
the Levites and brought them back to their temple duties.
Then he appointed four faithful men to take charge of the
money and produce collected, and to distribute it equitably
among their brethren in the ministry. Evidently there had
been no one previously who had been especially assigned to
look after this matter, which had been nominally under the
oversight of the high priest. Again Nehemiah closes the
paragraph with a brief prayer, requesting God not to forget
his zeal for the Lord's house and for its services.

Another abuse soon detected by Nehemiah was the careless desecration of the Sabbath day (vv. 15-22). He saw
country people treading the grapes in the winepresses on the
Sabbath. Others he observed hauling wine, grapes and figs
into the city on the holy day, and then selling this produce
in Jerusalem. Nehemiah records the fact that he warned
these people not to do such things any more on the Sabbath.
He also discovered Gentiles, men of Tyre, behaving in a
similar way by selling fish "and all manner of ware" to the
Jews. While it was permissible for Gentiles to dwell within

the city, it was not proper for them to break the Mosaic law by violating the Sabbath if they did so.

Once more Nehemiah contended with the nobles (the rulers) who had the responsibility for putting a stop to such practices. They probably had tolerated these illicit deeds because they enjoyed partaking of this fresh food themselves. Nehemiah reminded them that violation of the Sabbath was one of the principal sins which had previously brought down God's judgment on the nation. Because of such transgressions their ancestors had been expelled from the land (cf. Jer. 17:27).

The gates of the city also received Nehemiah's attention. Verse 19 speaks of the time when they "began to be dark before the sabbath." The Jews have always reckoned a day as running from sunset to sunset, based on the terminology in Genesis 1. As soon therefore as the shadows began to fall on the gates of Jerusalem, Nehemiah ordered them to be closed until the Sabbath was past. This of course most effectively prevented outside merchants from entering and hawking their wares. However, for a couple of weeks these people still kept on coming anyhow. Since they could not get inside Jerusalem, they camped just outside the gates until the time of opening on the next day. Such procedure caused commotion and disturbance which Nehemiah felt to be unseemly for the Sabbath. Therefore, he finally warned the merchants not to do so again, threatening that they would be thrown into prison, which brought the practice to a sudden end!

As a temporary measure, Nehemiah had his own servants take charge of the superintending of the gates (v. 19). Later he commanded the Levites to take over this responsibility. The paragraph describing these dealings closes with one of

Nehemiah's familiar brief prayers. Notice in this one that he did not expect God to save him on the basis of these good things he did, but rather he asked Him, "Spare me according to the greatness of thy mercy" (v. 22). This is reminiscent of the statement of the apostle in Titus 3:5: "Not by works of righteousness which we have done, but according to his mercy he saved us."

As he once more became familiar with the things going on in Judah, Nehemiah discovered that a number of the Jews had fallen into the sin of marrying "strange wives" (v. 27), women of Ammon, Moab and the Philistine city of Ashdod. The sad outcome was that their children were a mixture of heathen and Israelite, even in their very speech. The godly governor was filled with righteous indignation. Only a comparatively short time before, the people had solemnly covenanted before God not to do this thing. Nehemiah dealt with the matter with "characteristic roughness and force."[4] He cursed the offenders, struck them, even "plucked off their hair." Then he required them to swear an oath that they would do this no more.

In warning them he used a telling illustration, Solomon.[5] This wise and glorious monarch, so blessed of God; nevertheless fell into serious sin through the very same practice. He married "outlandish women." "Outlandish" is not here used in the modern sense of bizarre or grotesque, but of heathen women who were from outside the land. These women caused even Solomon to sin, and as a result the whole nation was rent in two with a schism from which it never recovered. Should Israel again rashly leap into such a trans-

---

[4] G. Campbell Morgan, *An Exposition of the Whole Bible*, p. 196.
[5] See I Kings 11.

gression, which had produced so much grief in earlier history?

One case of an especially flagrant character was uncovered by Nehemiah (vv. 28-31). A grandson of the high priest Eliashib had actually married a daughter of Sanballat, the governor of Samaria and great enemy of the Jews. Nehemiah says briefly but succinctly, "Therefore I chased him from me." Evidently this means that he altogether exiled the man from the land.

Josephus tells of a brother of Jaddua, the high priest, named Manasseh, who was forced out of his office because he married the daughter of Sanballat. He further states that Sanballat built a temple on Mount Gerizim, the highest peak in Samaria, appointing Manasseh to be the high priest there. This it seems was the commencement of the Samaritan worship which rivaled that of Jerusalem (see John 4:20). The only difficulty in aligning this account with the closing verses of Nehemiah is that Josephus dates the events at the time of the fall of the Persian Empire to Alexander the Great. However, it is claimed that in more than one place Josephus is known to be confused on chronology. It seems probable that his record is true except that it all took place in Nehemiah's day.[6]

"Remember them, O my God, because they have defiled the priesthood, and the covenant of the priesthood, and of the Levites" (v. 29). With these words Nehemiah followed his usual course of committing such things to the Lord for His dealing. The priests by careless, worldly conduct had "defiled the priesthood," the high office which God had committed to them.

[6] For an enlightening discussion of the matter see C. F. Keil and Franz Delitzsch, VIII, 295-96.

"Thus cleansed I them from all strangers" (v. 30). Probably this cleansing was accomplished by some such process as that described in the final chapter of Ezra. In addition Nehemiah saw to it that the priests and Levites were again performing their proper duties. He even made sure that the offerings of wood and of firstfruits were properly collected and taken care of.

"Remember me, O my God, for good." This brief prayer at the very end of the book is "a characteristic termination of a book whereof one of the main features has been a constant carrying to God of all the author's cares, troubles, and difficulties."[7] After a careful study of his book, we are left with a vivid impression of Nehemiah as a man of strong convictions and of forceful character. His ministry was not that of a teacher, but of a fearless, intrepid leader and hard worker. Whether dealing with friend or enemy he was always forthright and direct, often indeed to the point of bluntness and of what today probably would be called tactlessness. Pervading every atom of his being was a flaming zeal for the Lord and for His work. Even among those who have a real love for God and His Word such men are not often found. Oh, that God might raise up even a few in our own day, for once again the "walls" are crumbling and the foe is attacking!

---

[7] *Pulpit Commentary*, VII, 142.

BIBLIOGRAPHY

Archer, Gleason L., Jr. *A Survey of Old Testament Introduction.* Chicago: Moody, 1964.

Edersheim, Alfred. *The Temple: Its Ministry and Services.* London: Hodder and Stoughton, n.d.

Encyclopaedia Britannica. 11th Ed. Vol. II.

Fairbairn, Patrick (ed.). *Imperial Standard Bible Encyclopaedia.* Vol. II. Grand Rapids: Zondervan, 1957.

Free, Joseph P. *Archaeology and Bible History.* 5th ed., rev.; Wheaton, Ill.: Scripture Press, 1956.

Gaebelein, A. C. *The Annotated Bible.* Vol. III: *Ezra-Psalms.* New York: Loizeaux, n.d.

Gesenius, William. *Hebrew Lexicon.* Oxford: Clarendon, 1955.

Haley, John W. *An Examination of the Alleged Discrepancies of the Bible.* Nashville: Goodpasture, 1951.

Henry, Matthew. *Commentary on the Whole Bible.* Vol. II. Westwood, N.J.: Revell, n.d.

International Standard Bible Encyclopaedia. Grand Rapids: Eerdmans, 1949.

Ironside, H. A. *The Continual Burnt Offering.* New York: Loizeaux, 1941.

—————. *Notes on Ezra, Nehemiah and Esther.* New York: Loizeaux, n.d.

Jamieson, Robert; Fausset, A. R.; and Brown, David. *A Critical and Explanatory Commentary on the Old and New Testaments.* Grand Rapids: Eerdmans, 1948.

Josephus, Flavius. *Antiquities of the Jews*. Westwood, N.J.: Revell, n.d.

Keil, C. F. and Delitzsch, Franz. *Biblical Commentary on the Old Testament*. Vol. VIII: *The Books of Ezra, Nehemiah, Esther*. Edinburgh: T. & T. Clark, 1873.

Luck, G. Coleman. *The Bible Book by Book*. Chicago: Moody, 1955.

———. *Daniel*. Chicago: Moody, 1958.

Moorehead, W. G. *Studies in the Mosaic Institutions*. Grand Rapids: Kregel, 1957.

Morgan, G. Campbell. *An Exposition of the Whole Bible*. Westwood, N. J.: Revell, 1959.

Pulpit Commentary. H. D. M. Spence and J. S. Exell (eds.). Vol. VII. New York: Funk & Wagnalls, n.d.

Thompson, D. A. *Jerusalem and the Temples in Bible History and Prophecy*. London: Sov. Grace, n.d.

Unger, Merrill F. *Unger's Bible Dictionary*. Chicago: Moody, 1960.

Whitcomb, John C. *Darius the Mede*. Grand Rapids. Eerdmans, 1962.

Woodcock, P. G. *Concise Dictionary of Ancient History*. New York: Philosophical Lib., 1955.

Young, Robert. *Analytical Concordance to the Bible*. New York: Funk & Wagnalls, 1910.